DELIUS

as I knew him

ERIC FENBY

GREENWOOD PRESS, PUBLISHERS
WESTPORT, CONNECTICUT

Library of Congress Cataloging in Publication Data

Fenby, Eric, 1906-
    Delius as I knew him.

    Reprint of the 1948 ed. published by Quality
Press, London.
    Includes index.
    1. Delius, Frederick, 1862-1934.
[ML410.D35F4   1975]   780'.92'4 [B]   75-25255
ISBN 0-8371-8394-4

TO

MY FATHER AND MOTHER

WITH

GRATITUDE AND AFFECTION

This edition first published in 1948 by Quality Press, Ltd.,
London

Reprinted with the permission of Ernest Benn, Ltd.

Reprinted in 1975 by Greenwood Press, Inc.
51 Riverside Avenue, Westport, CT 06880

Library of Congress catalog card number 75-25255
ISBN 0-8371-8394-4

Printed in the United States of America

10 9 8 7 6 5 4 3 2

AUTHOR'S NOTE

M Y thanks are due to my friend James Gunn for his kindness in allowing me to reproduce the fine sketch in oils of Delius which forms the frontispiece of this book. This head must not be confused with the portrait to which reference is made on pp. 117–18. It represents the painter's first impression of the composer, an impression which, in my eyes, is the truest I have seen. I am grateful to Messrs. Boosey & Hawkes for their courtesy in permitting me to print extracts from the full scores of *A Song of Summer* and *Songs of Farewell*, and to the Universal Edition for a similar favour in respect of a quotation from the *Walk to the Paradise Garden*. I must also acknowledge the kindness of the following publishers in giving me their consent to quote from copyright works: Messrs. Allen & Unwin for various passages from Thomas Common's translation of Nietzsche's *Thus Spake Zarathustra*; Messrs. Dent & Sons for extracts from John of Ruysbroeck's *The Adornment of the Spiritual Marriage*; Messrs. Macmillan and the Executors of the late W. E. Henley for the poem " Margaritae Sorori "; Messrs. Chatto & Windus for several short extracts from Walt Whitman's *Leaves of Grass*. I am indebted to the B.B.C. for allowing me to reprint my description of the *Idyll* here, to Mr. Balfour Gardiner, and to the

AUTHOR'S NOTE

Executors of the late Frederick and Jelka Delius for permission to publish several letters, and, in addition, I respectfully ask the indulgence of those whom I have mentioned in my narrative.

E. F.

CONTENTS

PART ONE

AN INTERLUDE IN
THE LIFE OF FREDERICK DELIUS

I

YOUTH is a strange time, and the stuff of Youth is stranger. For some, for the coarser and happier natures among us, Youth is the playtime of Life; for others, for the more impressionable and thoughtful of us, Youth is a gradual and painful awakening to the sense of our heritage. We turn from one conflicting philosophy to another in our pathetic attempts to solve for ourselves the tremendous problem of Good and Evil, and, swept off our feet by violent enthusiasms, we oscillate between this and that conception of Life until, weary and dispirited, we look about us in this beautiful world and curse the day that man began to philosophise. Then there begins that passionate chase of all those transitory things that pall almost as soon as possessed. Puzzled and perplexed, we learn the World's Way:

> As, to behold Desert a beggar born,
> And needy Nothing trimm'd in jollity,
> And purest Faith unhappily forsworn,
> And gilded Honour shamefully misplaced,
> And maiden Virtue rudely strumpeted,
> And right Perfection wrongly disgraced,
> And Strength by limping Sway disabled,
> And Art made tongue-tied by Authority,
> And Folly, doctor-like, controlling Skill,
> And simple Truth miscall'd Simplicity,
> And captive Good attending captain Ill –

3

until, hopelessly disillusioned, we are left with our shattered ideals.

Yet there is one thing the world with all its rottenness cannot take from us, and that is the deep and abiding joy and consolation perpetuate in Great Music. Here the Spirit may find home and relief when all else fails. It offers an 'open sesame' to a world of contentment such as naught can offer in this brief sojourn here, until at last we shall be brought into the presence of that 'Eternal Light which loves and smiles.'

In my own experience the glorious final pages of Elgar's Second Symphony have given me a deeper insight into life, and kindled a greater zest for living, than all that philosophy has ever taught me. Here is the message of a man who had lived and found life hard but good, and every minute of it worth living. Yes, it had been good, but something even finer yet awaited him !

May he rest serene in the company of the Great Musician and the great masters of the noble art he served so well !

Here let those who would cavil remember that Elgar is the only English composer, probably the only composer, who has given perfect expression to that rarest and sublimest of all moods (and that but once for a few bars only at the beginning of the Second Part of his *Dream of Gerontius*) – the mood to which all composers should surely aspire, the mood which savours of that heavenly world wherein lies our destiny, whether we have the courage and honesty to admit it or not – the mood of blessed felicity, by which I mean an active and loving rest in God.

This is far removed from sanctimoniousness, but surely we of this tired world need such music of rest and felicity as never before.

The debt of humanity to its Great Music-Makers can never be paid, and, though most of them went hungry of the things of this world, their meed is not to be reckoned in gold.

It was in such a mood of intense gratitude for all the loveliness Frederick Delius had brought into my life that I first wrote to him, in the hope that it might give him pleasure to know that his music had meant so much in the life of a very young man.

As yet, I had heard none of his music in the concert-room except an atrocious performance of his Violin Concerto, the violin-pianoforte arrangement of which had been done to death by two of our local celebrities. It says much for my tender enthusiasm of those days for Delius's music that it too was not quenched by such a rendering. I had had, therefore, to content myself with the occasional broadcast performances of his work, and with such gramophone records as had then been issued.

In Yorkshire, the county of his birth, it was almost impossible to find out anything about his published music, and, had this been possible, the purchase of but a few scores would have emptied my slender purse at that time.

Nevertheless, I had known on first hearing it that the music of this man was no ordinary music. It had moved me so strangely and unaccountably, and this even at second-hand, so to speak.

When, at last, after weeks of enquiries and dis-
appointments, I was able to peruse the vocal score
of his *Mass of Life*, I had stood spellbound in the little
music-shop in the main street of my native town as I
read that soul-stirring and original passage for Solo
Contralto which, rendered into English by Thomas
Common, reads:

> O Zarathustra ! Beyond good and evil found we our
> island and our green meadow – we two alone !
> Therefore must we be friendly to each other !
> . . . O Zarathustra, thou
> art not faithful enough to me !
>
> .   .   .   .
>
> There is an old heavy, heavy, booming-clock: it
> boometh by night up to thy cave: –
>
> – When thou hearest this clock strike the hours at
> midnight, then thinkest thou between one and twelve
> thereon –
> – Thou thinkest thereon, O Zarathustra, I know it
> – of soon leaving me ! –

As I read on, a cold thrill ran through me at the
magical entry of the chorus basses singing *sotto voce*:

> O man ! Take heed !
> What saith deep midnight's voice indeed ?
> 'I slept my sleep –
> From deepest dream I've woke and plead: –
> The world is deep,
> And deeper than the day could read.
> Deep is its woe –
> Joy – deeper still than grief can be:
> Woe saith: Hence ! Go !
> But joys all want eternity –
> Want deep, profound eternity !'

and my musing continued until long after the Solo
Soprano's tender and exquisite close:

And we gazed at each other, and looked at the green meadow o'er which the cool evening was just passing, and we wept together.

I knew nothing of Nietzsche. It was the music that struck me to the heart so that I could scarcely think of anything else for days.

Thus, by the merest chance, on my first handling a Delius score, I stumbled on the very pages that contain the musical pith of all the composer had to say.

. . . .

I had not expected to receive any acknowledgment of my letter, and was greatly surprised to hear from Delius as follows:

> 'Grez-sur-Loing,
> 'Bourron,
> 'France.
> '9.6.1928.

'My dear young friend, — Your sympathetic and appreciative letter gave me the greatest pleasure. I am always glad when I hear that my music appeals to the young. I know Scarborough quite well; when a schoolboy I used to spend my summer holidays at Filey and my memories of all the happy days on that coast are still very green. Most likely the Philharmonic choir will give the *Mass of Life* again under Kennedy Scott next year, when perhaps you may be able to hear it.

> 'With warm greetings,
> 'I remain,
> 'Sincerely yours,
> 'Frederick Delius.'

About this time I had read several articles on Delius and his music, and had learnt of his unhappy plight, namely that he was now blind and paralysed and unable to work any more. But the real tragedy of it all, or so it seemed to me, was to hear that the composer was worried and unhappy because it was physically impossible for him to continue and finish his life's work. Apparently there were several works which he had begun, and been unable to complete. He could bear with his misfortunes if only he could finish these scores.

To have something beautiful in you and not be able to bring it to fruition because the human machinery had broken down seemed hard. To be a genius, as this man plainly was, and have something beautiful in you and not be able to rid yourself of it because you could no longer see your score paper and no longer hold your pen – well, the thought was unbearable !

I remember how, with my dog, Peter, I walked for miles one stormy day on the cliffs reflecting on the helplessness and misery of the man. What delicacy of feeling was in his music ! What must such a sensitive nature be suffering ? Could not anything be done ? Of course, I would be willing to—— But how dare I presume such a thing ! It was preposterous ! Ashamed and surprised, I dismissed the idea from my mind and, battling with the wind, tried to think of other things.

During the next few weeks the conceit that I could help became an obsession. It chased me like some Hound of Heaven, and I hid from it under any and every excuse that I could find; but it was always there, and in the end I could not sleep for it. Finally it conquered me, and, getting up in the middle of the night, I took pen and paper and wrote to Delius offering my help for three or four years. I would do anything to be the means of his finishing that music, and, provided that my suggestion was acceptable to him at all, I felt certain that I would succeed in my purpose. How it was going to be done – well, God alone knew the answer to that !

I told no one, and waited anxiously for his reply. It came:

'Grez-sur-Loing,
'Bourron,
'29.8.1928.

'DEAR MR. FENBY, – I am greatly touched by your kind and sympathetic letter and I should love to accept your offer. Come here by all means as soon as you can and see if you like it before deciding anything. How old are you ?

'You know, this is a lovely spot, just a quiet little village and our house is in a big garden going down to the river, but of course we live very much alone.

'Perhaps the best way for you to come would be to travel from London during the night. For instance – you take the train at 9.10 a.m. to Bourron, our station, where you will be at 11 and where we will have you fetched if we know when to expect you. With kind regards from my wife,

'I am,
'Yours sincerely,
'FREDERICK DELIUS.'

Then followed some correspondence concerning passports, and I received a postcard from Mrs. Delius

informing me that Delius's *Sea-drift* was to be performed at the Leeds Festival, and that if I had not
arranged to leave before that date her husband would
like me to hear it.

I went over to Leeds at the last moment, but, owing
to the stupidity of a minor official, I was unable to
gain admittance in spite of the fact that I offered ten
shillings to be privileged to stand inside the door at
the back of the hall for that one piece.

However, I was able to tell Delius that I had heard
on good authority that Sir Thomas Beecham had
excelled himself, and given a magnificent performance.

Some months later, when I met Sir Thomas at
Grez, he chaffed me about my adventure. 'My dear
boy,' said he, 'if I had only known I would have put
you on the platform !'

The last letter from Grez before my departure read:

'1.10.1928.

'DEAR MR. FENBY, – My husband was very pleased
with your letter and said you did quite right with the
Passport authorities. . . . I hope your journey will
not be delayed as we are expecting our great friend
Balfour Gardiner on the 20th and he is anxious to play
an arrangement of a Delius work with you which he
has made. You would have to copy out your part
from his manuscript. So you see your kind help will
be required at once.

'With kindest regards from us both, also to your
parents,

'Yours sincerely,
'JELKA DELIUS.

'P.S. – I will meet you in Bourron.'

2

I T had rained all night, and when the train steamed into the long and straggling station of the lazy little village of Bourron, a half-hour's walk over the fields from Grez-sur-Loing, that October morning, there seemed to be no duller place on earth. It was still drizzling when I alighted, and I looked about me for some friendly recognition. It came from a rather unexpected face, and I found myself saying, 'Mrs. Delius – I presume?' I saw that she was surprised, and this, I afterwards learnt, was due to my absurdly young appearance. We shook hands, and a soft and unusual voice with a slightly un-English accent about it greeted me: 'Mr. Fenby, this is a pleasure! I am so delighted that you have come out here to help my husband. We both appreciate your kindness very much. If only you can work together in some way it will be so good for him, better than all the medicines in the world, and it is the dream of my life that he will be able to compose again.'

She instructed André, the untidy little chauffeur, to collect my things, and as we walked down the platform I saw that she had kind eyes. She was dressed simply, of fair complexion and medium height, amply proportioned and obviously a woman of great physical strength.

We climbed up into the ancient Ford with its

yellow curtains, a lovable old bone-shaker familiar to unknown visitors as the Delius ensign at the railway station, and were soon on our way down the station lane. This grand old chariot had never failed them. In its heyday they had toured Italy in it, but now it did no manner of work for six days, but on the seventh day, Friday, out it came to take them off to market. It remained their trusty servant until a few months before Mrs. Delius's death, when it was sold to the chauffeur. But such was its devotion to the Delius household that it had no mind to serve others, not even the little fellow who had tended it with such care for years. It had taken the hill over to Fontainebleau a thousand and one times with all the impudence of a Bluebird, but on its first outing with its new master it had not the heart to mount it. Half-way up the hill it refused to go an inch farther, and then it ran backwards, mounted the kerb, and smashed itself up on its side !

We now struck the *grande-route*, passing beneath a long avenue of tall and stately poplars which stretched away over the hill-top like some proud regiment in double file. This noble bodyguard was felled to the ground some months afterwards with all the ruthlessness of the modern State behind each blow, and now, eight years later, the fresh young trees cannot quite dispel the sense of desolation about the place, nor take from my heart the sound of those dying groans.

The last moan of a tree as it falls to the ground is one of the saddest sounds I know.

I asked how Delius was, and was told that he was fairly well, that he was still resting, and that he would be brought downstairs at mid-day to see me. Mrs. Delius hoped that I played the piano, as they were expecting a visit from a great friend of theirs, a Russian 'cellist named Barjansky, who would be sure to bring his instrument along with him.

With this we turned to the left, down a lane, and, having passed a vulgar and pretentious villa, gaily coloured and adorned with hogs' heads, my companion said, 'This is Grez. We have lived here for over thirty years!'

We entered the village, which seemed none too clean, all grey and depressing, and zigzagging our way through the narrow streets we finally halted outside the rambling house which was to be my home for the greater part of the next six years.

It was a curious house, fronting the street and divided in the middle by a great porch through which one could have driven a loaded hay-waggon with ease. Over this porch was a corridor, which joined the two wings of the house together, and here Delius's German male nurse had his room. In the right wing there was a big living-room, beyond it the kitchen, and overhead Delius's bedroom and a guest-room. In the left wing there was a guest-room on the street level, and upstairs the music-room, which led into a small but lofty bedroom. This was to be my room. Over the two wings were enormous studios, and branching out from the side of the right wing was yet another studio with glass roof, whilst underneath it were the various outhouses. The back of the house looked on to a now faded garden, and in the background, some two to three hundred yards away, the great trees by the river-side piled themselves up in a gigantic semicircle, but with a mellowness about them such as I had never seen before.

We climbed the stairs up to the music-room, and, pausing in the doorway, Mrs. Delius said, 'This is the room where Delius has written all his finest music.'

I entered with reverence. Immediately I felt the atmosphere was somewhat sinister, and I was curiously ill at ease. To the very end of my days in Grez I never fully overcame that unpleasant feeling in the music-room. Sometimes, when I have been hundreds of miles away, I have suddenly remembered it and shuddered. I cannot understand it at all.

It was a long room, with two heavily curtained windows looking down on to the street, and one on to the garden. Taking my eyes off the Ibach grand piano at which Delius had composed, I glanced from picture to picture on the yellow walls. Instantly I felt a distaste for those sickly pinks which had been lavished on almost every canvas, and, fearing lest my dislike should be observed, I turned my attention to the crowded bookshelves.

'Look, Mr. Fenby, this is your room through here. I hope you will be comfortable,' continued Mrs. Delius. 'I will go and tell Delius that you are here, and will call you when he is ready.'

I was now left alone. A full-sized face of mad Strindberg by Munch frowned down at me from over the foot of the bed, and over the head was a framed photograph of Nietzsche. More fantastic creations of Munch, dark with suicide, hung high up on the walls, which were covered by a coarse brown material (almost like sacking) held by tacks, and round the wainscot had been stencilled quaint little hunting scenes. Over by the window to the garden was a clever little sketch of a shrieking goblin. Could this be the fellow who sometimes shouts in the wrong place in *Eventyr*?

It was all so strange that I wondered whether I should have nightmare that night. But I longed to see Delius, and was only happy, though a little nervous, when at last I stood hesitating on the door-step of the living-room which led from the porch.

'Here is Mr. Fenby,' prompted his wife.

'Come in, come in, Fenby. I am very glad to meet you,' said Delius, and I walked slowly across the room to return his greeting.

Nothing can ever dim the memory of that first meeting.

There was Delius, gaunt, deathly pale, his fine classical head proud and erect as he sat upright in his chair. Round him stretched a great screen so that for a moment it seemed as if some Roman Cardinal was sitting there. He wore a white shirt open at the neck, and a checked rug hung loosely about his knees. With difficulty he extended his arm, as though to compel the life to return into his drooping hand. Again I hesitated. It seemed wrong to shake hands, but a glance from Mrs. Delius reassured me. I took the long tapering fingers in mine, and in words something like these I said, 'Well, sir, this is a very great honour. I am very proud and privileged to

come here, and it is very good of you to receive me so
kindly.'

'Now, Fenby,' said Delius, 'just make yourself at
home, and use everything in your part of the house as
if it were your own – my music, my music-room.
But sit down and tell me about your journey.'

We talked about Scarborough, which he had known
very well as a boy. Did I go to the Cricket Festivals
as he had done ? Did I know Filey ? What glorious
times he had had there when his family used to take
a house in the Crescent for the summer holidays !
How he loved playing cricket in the neighbouring
villages of Gristhorpe and Hunmanby, and what fine
fellows the farm-hands were ! He had nearly lost
his life in some mad escapade on the Brigg when,
along with another boy, he had been trapped by the
tide.

The conversation flowed pleasantly and easily
enough until it suddenly turned to music – English
music – how, I cannot remember. But I shall never
forget the change that came over him when, in my
innocence, I uttered these two harmless words, nor
shall I forget that frown, that contemptuous smile,
which he rounded off by a sly pursing of the lips in a
manner peculiarly his own, that smile which I grew
to anticipate whenever visitors began skating on thin
ice, nor that startling, almost uncouth broadness of
speech as he interrupted me: 'English music ? Did
you say English music ?' There was a pause, and
then he added, 'Well – I've never heard of any !'

What had I said ? I felt the blood flow to my
finger-tips, and in the silence which followed I saw

many things, but, clearest of all, that if I was to stay
here for months on end and work with him I must not
voice my opinions.

The immensity of my self-imposed task weighed
hard upon me, and I could have given it up there and
then but for my pride. He remained silent, and did
not address me until his wife and I were seated for
lunch, and then he merely asked me what I would
drink. I was thankful when we had finished, for all
through the meal he continued severe and aloof, and
I felt that every word of our conversation, hers and
mine, had been a word too many for him. He had
endured it, and had now and then broken the silence
with, 'Bitte, Brod. . . . Kartoffeln. . . . Spinat. . . .
Geben Sie mir mein Bier' – but this not for us, but
for the young German nurse who was feeding him.

When I rose to go, he told me that on his desk in
the music-room I should find the MS. score of an
unpublished work of his – a symphonic poem, *A
Poem of Life and Love* – and that he wanted me to
transcribe it into short score so that it could be played
on two pianos. He would like to hear it again, to see
if it was good. His friend, Balfour Gardiner, had
already begun it; would I finish it ?

I lit my pipe and read through the score; I was
hopelessly disappointed. It was true there were
lovely passages here and there, but the work might
have been written by a student in Delius's manner.
Turning to the last page of Gardiner's arrangement, I
began to work. Two hours later three strokes on the
bell called me down to tea, and as I approached the
door I heard the young German reading aloud. The

reading stopped as I entered and Mrs. Delius came to my rescue. Happily, there was no need for that kindness, for Delius had evidently made up his mind to be entertaining just as I had made up mine to avoid the mention of music like the plague.

I trembled to think what I would say should he ask for my opinion on that symphonic poem !

After tea we left them to their reading, and Mrs. Delius and I walked down the garden. Here I learnt the routine of the household; how that one could take out one's watch at any hour of the day and say, 'It is half-past eleven – at this moment the nurse will be carrying Delius downstairs'; or, 'It is two o'clock – they will be taking him upstairs to rest'; or, 'It is half-past five – Mrs. Delius will just be relieving the German nurse'; or, 'It is three in the morning – the nurse will be lifting him up to give him his orangeade' – and all this with an almost military precision.

I found conversation a little trying, for my mind was full of anxieties. Would I settle ? Had I it in me to accustom myself to the conditions of this strange household ? I did not fear loneliness, but could I stand the complete lack of young society for months at a time in such a place as this ?

I dreaded going indoors to that music-room; but that was nothing. How could I work with such a difficult man as Delius ? The dankness of the garden oppressed me, and when two strokes of the bell sounded – for Mrs. Delius to go in and take her turn in the eternal round of reading aloud – I went out into the street to explore the village.

It was already dark, and too dark to make out much

of the church, except that there was a fine tower which jutted out over the street, sheltering the pavement. I passed beneath it and took the road before me. Two men returning from the fields bade me 'Bon-soir,' and as I sauntered by the cottages I smelt delicious soups in the making, for they were preparing the evening meal.

The full significance of my undertaking became a sober reality and not a dream any more, and, looking up into the starry heavens, I prayed that I might succeed. It is hard to pray at any time, and harder still to an accompaniment of barking dogs, for my unfamiliar steps had aroused the great Alsatians in a yard near by, and soon it seemed as if the dogs of the whole countryside were raging against me, such a barking and a yapping was there. In a lighter mood I should have taken heart from this welcome, but I was sad in the darkness and a little afraid.

I turned, and, entering the house, crept upstairs to the music-room and resumed my work.

At seven o'clock, Hildegarde, the pretty young Saxon maid, came in shyly and said, 'Wollen Sie bitte zum essen kommen?' – so I went downstairs to supper.

The good food, the wine, and the delightful conversation revived me, and my heart went out to these two dear old people. The old man's humanity returned to him, and he became irresistible, and I saw much that was sweet and lovable in his wife.

After supper, with a flickering oil-lamp to guide us, we pushed him in his carriage up a hill which led out of the village, and which, they told me, would take one over to Marlotte, where lived old Joe Heseltine, an uncle of Philip. So long as the weather was favourable Delius never missed this airing before retiring. The cool evening air was fresh and delicious and everything was at peace. Little was said, and we left him to his thoughts. We met no one on the way, and, as we retraced our steps and neared the village, the street lights went out – for it was nine o'clock and the village was already asleep.

Bidding them 'Good night,' I went up to my room and remembered no more until I heard a voice calling, 'Voila l'eau chaude, monsieur.'

It was eight o'clock, and the beginning of my first full day in Grez.

3

WHEN I had taken my coffee and rolls I went out into the garden, and, finding Mrs. Delius there, I wandered down to the river with her and heard the news.

Delius had slept well, and was free from pain. He had not called her to read aloud in the night; that was a good sign. Barjansky would be here for supper, and would probably be staying for two nights. The visits of such great artists as this 'cellist were all too rare, and, so long as Delius could bear the strain of listening intently, such intimate music-makings as they enjoyed on these occasions made him as happy as he could ever expect to be. But one could never be sure of him; he was such a physical wreck, and had to be watched and cared for as a baby in arms. The slightest thing, no matter how trivial it might be, upset him, for he had no strength to fight against it. There were weeks when he would never so much as mention music at all, nor even ask for a gramophone record of his own music to be played to him; weeks when he just trailed on from day to day, eating a little and drinking out of all proportion to the next-to-nothing he ate, when he did little else but sleep, and this even during the reading. This distressing state of apathy had greatly worried Mrs. Delius, and she had longed to have some young and enthusiastic musician about the house to rekindle his interest. She had written to Philip Heseltine asking him to come and live with them, but he had been unable to do so, and when they had received my letter she had grasped at the opportunity with both hands. It had seemed a heaven-sent blessing. Now she was happy, and, if only the public appreciation of her husband's music would quicken and become vital, she would have all that she could desire. It saddened her to think that this beautiful and original music – the work of a lifetime – was being so shamefully neglected. It would be harder still if on his death there was a sudden vogue for it.

However, Delius had been very definite that morning. He had said that he particularly wanted Barjansky to play him his 'Cello Concerto and Sonata, and that I was to look at the piano parts of these works.

There was something of a command in that tone, and I went in mortal dread of it, for these works were but names to me.

I was so anxious to begin my practising at once that I took little notice of the church, which I saw was early Norman, on the one side of the house, or the ruined tower on the other; but the recollection of those great and majestic Italian poplars higher up the river compelled me to gaze at them again from the music-room window before sitting down to my formidable task. I practised until lunch and my confidence came back to me.

Delius was very talkative and happy, for my delight in his 'Cello Sonata was unrestrained. I could not forget those soaring melodies, nor the subtleties of their accompaniments. The treatment was mostly chordal, it is true, but the placing of the chords was so sensitive, so pregnant with suggestion, that, as each new phrase bred in its stride the next phrase, one's soul took flight along with it. I was impatient over my food, for I hungered after more of that rhapsody. Such music is the food of the Spirit, which cannot be so easily appeased.

I played on until tea-time, and, when Mrs. Delius suggested that instead of reading aloud to him Delius might care to hear a gramophone record, I thrilled with expectancy, for it is always a fascinating thing to observe the effect of a man's music on himself. He chose Sir Thomas Beecham's beautiful record of his *On Hearing the First Cuckoo in Spring*, and, sitting there opposite him in the quiet of that great room, with no fidgeting neighbours or disturbing faces to distract, one touched the very heart of Music in those exquisite opening bars. Never had the sound of strings nor Goossens's oboe-playing seemed so magical ! A curious other-worldliness possessed him. With his head thrown back, and swaying slightly to the rhythm, he seemed to be seeing with those now wide-open yet unseeing eyes, and his spirit ebbed and flowed with the rise and fall of his music.

There was nothing of the quietist's surrender to idle activity here, nor the sensualist's love of mere sound, out a continued reaching out of himself. A great mystic has said that 'God is an ocean that ebbs and flows,' and no words are truer than these of Great Music. It is only when we are unconscious of the pulse of Time that we can aspire through goodness to

be at one with Things Eternal. The pause at the
turning of the disc did not disturb his rapture, and
this going-out of himself through the noble love of
music continued until after the lovely sounds of that
final and singularly beautiful cadence had died away.
Not until those moments of silence immediately following that music did I realise to the full the utter
poverty of words when, reverting to mortal speech, I
fished about in my mind for something to say. We
have all of us heard the inane remarks that people
have made at such times, and I have come to dread
these moments, for they invariably take away from us
all that we have received. Guided by a wiser impulse,
I let the silence speak for me, and in a quiet voice I
added two words only: 'Thank you.' He made no
response, and, smiling at his wife, I rose and stole
gently out of the room.

When I came down to supper that evening, Barjansky was there. I was not prepared to find so unusual-
looking a man. He was of medium height, pale and
thin, but he had a striking head, with high forehead
and a mass of long bushy hair; but for his white shirt
he was dressed entirely in black, and wore black
gaiters like those of an Anglican dean. After a few
minutes' conversation with him I perceived him to be
an extremely likeable fellow, and one of those rare
musicians who give the impression of being musical.
He was evidently a great lover of Delius's work, and
his manner of address was born of reverence. He told
us, amongst other things, that the 'Cello Sonata had
been well received on his tour, that the quality of
German orchestras had much improved since Delius's

active days; and there was much questioning about far-off friends.

After supper Mrs. Delius reminded us that in a few minutes' time Sir Thomas Beecham would be broadcasting *Brigg Fair*. We heard it to perfection, and only once did it show signs of fading. When the music had ceased, Delius called out, 'Splendid, Thomas! That is how I want my music to be played. Beecham is the only conductor who has got the hang of it! That was a beautiful performance! . . . Now let's clear the air and play that record of the Revellers – "Ol' Man River."'

This and other such records gave him great pleasure, for the singing was reminiscent of the way his negroes used to sing out in Florida, when as a young orange-planter he had often sat up far into the night, smoking cigar after cigar, and listening to their subtle improvisations in harmony. 'They showed a truly wonderful sense of musicianship and harmonic resource in the instinctive way in which they treated a melody,' he added, 'and, hearing their singing in such romantic surroundings, it was then and there that I first felt the urge to express myself in music.'

The greater part of the following day was spent in vigorous rehearsal, and I was much amused by Barjansky, who would practise like a demon for an hour or so and then suddenly stop and say, 'Fenby, I must now take my repose.' Bathed in perspiration, he would then retire behind his 'cello-case, strip, dry his shirt before the stove, and, flinging himself in a state of the greatest exhaustion on the divan, would smoke the vilest cigarettes imaginable. He was a

C

most inspiring person, and played like an angel. As
the hours passed by my two battle-horses became
more manageable, and I was not thrown so often.
Barjansky was satisfied, and I resolved to hang on at
all costs, even by their tails if need be.

Six o'clock came and Delius was carried up to the
music-room. I could see that Barjansky was very
nervous, and I had never known such an ordeal, for
my future at Grez depended on it. We played. When
we had finished, Delius, all smiles and exultant,
shouted from his corner, 'Bravo, Barjansky ! It was
glorious. Nobody plays this work like you. Oh, it
was superb ! Bravo, Fenby ! You amaze me, my
boy. I am so glad to have you here with me.'

This reassured me on my difficult enterprise. We
excelled ourselves in the concerto, and the old man
said that we must have a bottle of Pol Roger up from
the cellar to celebrate at supper. When they had
carried him away and I was left alone with Barjansky,
he took my hand and said, 'Fenby, you are artiste.
It is vonderful for you that you are here; it is vonderful
for Delius.' I was overjoyed, for now it seemed to
me that what I had dared to dream two months before
on those distant cliffs of Yorkshire might yet be
achievable, and that I might gradually grow in his
musical favour until at last Delius would have
sufficient confidence in me to dictate to me.

After supper he asked for more music. Would we
play him some of the *Mass of Life* ? Opening the
doors of the long corridor to the music-room, they
propped him up in bed, and we played all we could
in terms of 'cello and piano, and when we were tired

and had come to the end, and had gone through to his room and heard his, 'What pleasure you two have given me to-day!' we were happy and contented and ready for sleep.

The next morning Barjansky left for Italy, and, as news came that Balfour Gardiner would be with us that evening, I took up the arrangement for two pianos of the symphonic poem and worked feverishly.

That day at lunch Delius said, 'You will like Balfour. He is one of my oldest friends, and one of the very few people I trust and admire implicitly.' He then went on to tell me, with many a touch of dry humour, that Gardiner had given up music; that he had a theory that at a certain age a man ceases to be musical, and Gardiner had already reached that age.

'Would that many others thought the same,' said Delius.

He, Gardiner, now found much more fun in planting trees and painting rain-water tubs than in writing music. In fact, he had even been known to curtail a holiday and race across Europe to assist at the *accouchement* of his sow!

Delius was right. I did like Gardiner. I liked everything about him except his musical pessimism, and this I found intolerable. He could not see how Delius could possibly work again, yet he thought there was no harm in playing over that arrangement to him. I could understand his diffidence here, but I could not share his gloomy outlook on the future of music. Since then, however, I have not been free from such pessimism myself. Music as an art is a glorious thing, but music as a profession is an anathema. No man should follow it unless he can help it.

We played the arrangement through several times, but Delius merely thanked us and made no comment. After all, it seemed hopeless. Happily for me, Mrs. Delius still believed that something could be done.

4

No further mention of *A Poem of Life and Love* was made during the days which followed Balfour Gardiner's departure, and I tried hard to convince myself that this was because Delius was suffering more than usual. There were intervals when he was entirely free from pain, but there were long periods when a man of weaker fibre would have wished himself dead. Yet it was strange that he should never refer to that music, and I wondered what was going on in his mind. It distressed me deeply to see a man in such pain, and more than once the sight of it drove me from the room, such was his agony. But, since I had offered to take a turn with the reading to allow the others some recreation, and it had quickly become a habit that I should read regularly each day, I could not play the coward and run away.

Sir Thomas Beecham has said more than once that he could scarcely bear to see Delius at the latter part of his life, and that his visits to Grez always depressed him. What would he have felt had he witnessed those excruciating moments?

At such times – and it was so often towards sunset – Delius would suddenly become restless and uneasy, now wanting a thick rug over his legs, now a thin one, now no rug at all. Perhaps he would feel more comfortable with his feet on the ground? No, he had felt more relief with them on the chair. Were his feet touching ? Were his legs straight ? After half an hour or so of these preliminaries, during which one had been trying to read aloud to him, the pains in his legs would gradually intensify until his ravings became pitiful. Unbelievable though it may seem, I never once heard him complain, and the nobility and patience with which he bore his sufferings continually astonished me. It was hard to stand by and be so helpless, or to go on reading, as he always insisted that I should do, when it seemed that at any moment his struggles would end in his falling out of his great chair. Finally he would give in, and with difficulty and reluctance be carried off to bed. Every cure and every remedy had been tried in vain. Allopathic medicine made him worse. His only crumb of comfort was the calming influence of certain homœopathic remedies.

One thing was ever uppermost in my mind at Grez, and that was that only there, and with such constant care as his wife lavished on him, could he go on living. Her name deserves a very prominent place on the scroll of those who have given themselves unstintingly for others.

And so the days passed by uneventfully, and I found myself watching him as anxiously as the others. During those periods when Delius was suffering more than usual he could bear pain, but he could not endure the sound of conversation, and we ate and exchanged the usual politenesses of the table in silence. The slightest rattle of a cup or clatter of a spoon was sufficient to lash him into a fury, and if one forgot oneself and found oneself saying, 'Mrs. Delius, may I pass you so-and-so ?' it was certain to meet with his, 'Will you please be quiet !' The nervous tension one felt in his presence was almost unbearable, and, after sitting beside him for an hour, one left the room feeling as if one had been drained of one's life-blood. The house at such times resembled a tomb from which the living in it could have no hope of escape.

Then came a brighter day, when the sufferer was left in peace.

That evening, after supper, Delius surprised me by saying that he had an idea in his mind – a simple little tune – and that he wanted me to take it down.

I took paper and pen and waited eagerly. I had no idea what he would do – whether he would sing, or call out the names of the notes and their varying time-values. What he did was to stagger and confound me so utterly that I did not recover for the rest of that night.

Throwing his head back, he began to drawl in a loud monotone that was little more than the crudest extension of speech, and which, when there was anything of a ring about it, wavered round a tenor middle B. This is something like what I heard:

'Ter-te-ter – ter-te-ter – ter-te-te-ter' – and here he interjected 'Hold it !' and then went on – 'ter-te-te-ter – ter-ter-ter – te-ter – hold it ! – ter-te-te-ter – ter-ter-te-te-te-ter – hold it ! – ter-te-ter-ter-te-ter-ter-te-ter – hold it ! – ter-te-ter-ter-te-ter-ter-te-ter——'

Instantly my mind went back to those days in the Great War when, as a small boy, I had been accompanist in a concert party and had gone off almost every night to entertain the soldiers. Two or three items were always reserved for such 'Tommies' as cared to sing, and I had learnt something of the good-natured fellow who would come beaming up to the platform and whisper in one's ear, 'I haven't any music, but it goes like this: High-tee-tigh-tee-tigh-tee-tigh!'

When he had finished this amazing recital, he turned to me and asked, 'Have you got that? Now sing it!' I was dumbfounded.

'But – Delius,' I stammered, 'what key is it in?'

'A minor,' came the answer.

In a flash I saw that he evidently heard the tune imaginatively, but was unable to sing it.

'Well, we will try again,' he went on, and there was more suggestion of disgust and impatience in his tone than I cared to admit. It was obvious that he failed to understand how I could be so stupid.

I had observed that he disliked anything in the form of repetition – whether it were musical or verbal – and that if one had the misfortune to repeat oneself, one was never allowed to proceed very far. Unnecessary repetition annoyed him, and he sat there, tossing his head from side to side, and champing and frowning in his anger. This he always did when things went wrong. When I suggested that it would help me if he would call out the names of the notes, he gave a great sigh and added, 'Well, all right then!'

The drawling began again, but now on another note!

'A – BC – BD – E,' etc.

I quickly sketched the shape of this melody,[1] but had no idea of the stresses, nor even the time signature. I was too flurried, too nervous, too upset to go about it in the proper way. I had not thought that it would be like this, and the sting of my emotion pierced me to the heart. My pen flopped about in my fingers, and in my confusion I found myself holding it upside down. My fingers were inky, and the tears that I had been fighting to keep back now blurred my spectacles, and I could not see. The more I looked at this relic of a man, and heard his hopeless attempts to make himself understood in but the rudiments of the glorious art in which he so greatly excelled, the more distressed I became, until in the end the sight and sound of it were too much for me, and I broke down. I had to give it up !

Just then Mrs. Delius entered the room, and I pulled myself together as best I could and said, 'I am sorry, I cannot go on ! Please excuse me.'

I got up and went out into the porch, and as I groped my way in the pitch darkness round to the door which led up from the garden to the music-room, I overheard Delius say, 'Jelka, that boy is no good ! He is too slow. He cannot even take down a simple melody !'

I slept very little that night, for now it seemed that my mission was a complete fiasco. There was only one consolation, and that was in the thought that nobody on earth could have made head or tail of those faltering sounds.

---

[1] This melody, transposed into G minor, is now to be found in the second movement of Delius's Third Sonata for Violin and Piano.

The next day Delius was particularly kind to me, and I assumed that his wife must have told him something of the overwrought state in which she had found me. He was being wheeled about in the garden before lunch, when he sent for me and immediately began to discuss *A Poem of Life and Love*.

'My boy,' said he, 'I want you to look at that score, and tell me exactly what you think about it. Take your time, and when you are ready I will come up to the music-room, and you must play it, and then I will hear what you have to say.'

I was greatly astonished, yet not much comforted, for it will be remembered that I did not think well of this work, nor did I see how I could possibly tell him so. But later in the day, when I had talked over the difficult and embarrassing situation with Mrs. Delius, all she said was, 'Mr. Fenby, you must tell him exactly what you feel. After all, you are the only musician who is likely to be here for some considerable time, and, though I have no technical knowledge to say whether you are right or wrong, I do believe in you. You must forget your youth and stand up to him. I will always stand by you !

Be it to her eternal credit that, without this woman's belief that ultimately I should succeed in my purpose, my position at Grez during those early days would have been an impossible one. Never once did she waver in giving me her whole-hearted support.

I now made up my mind that I would assert myself at all costs, even if it ended by my being packed off bag and baggage to England ! On the following afternoon Delius was carried up to the music-room, and I struggled through the score at the piano. There was so much going on that it was a physical impossibility to play it with one pair of hands, but I called out the orchestration as best I could to refresh his memory, for he had not seen the full score for eight years. It was one of the last scores on which he had worked before he became totally blind.

I soon warmed up to my difficult task, and found myself criticising the work fearlessly. My first unfavourable comment electrified him, but it was not long before he saw my view and agreed with my opinion. Had I then known to what degree he resented severe criticism of his music, no man, nor even a woman, could have persuaded me to say what I did on that occasion. As we neared the end he stopped me and said, 'Look here, Fenby, I have got an idea. Select all the good material, develop it, and make a piece out of it yourself. Now, take your time; never hurry your work, whatever you do !'

This insistence on one's taking one's time was a point which I have heard him stress, over and over again, as of the greatest importance in all fine work. How could one always see at first sight the possibilities dormant in an idea, and relevant to the feelings one wanted to express ? He told me that though one could never foresee precisely what the finished work would be like, yet one should always have some definite goal in mind, and never take one's eyes off it. Whether one achieved it or not, of course, was another matter. Yet good work always shaped itself according to the laws of its own inner being.

'For instance,' said he, 'take *Sea-drift*, which, I

think, is one of my best works. The shape of it was taken out of my hands, so to speak, as I worked, and was bred easily and effortlessly of the nature and sequence of my particular musical ideas, and the nature and sequence of the particular poetical ideas of Whitman that appealed to me. Avoid all "fillings" and meaningless "passage-work," and remember what I say about taking your time.'

With this he called his nurse to carry him downstairs, and left me to my score. I smoked innumerable pipes over it during the hours which followed, and the next morning I took a long walk in the woods alone, turning over all that music in my mind.

It was fortunate for me that Delius had come up to the music-room without delay, for that day his sufferings returned, and again he was racked with pain. Now, I rarely visited his part of the house, except for meals, or to take my turn with the reading. For the next few days I delighted in working out his beautiful ideas with all the fascination of a chess problem. Then I left them, and thought no more about them, until one night shortly afterwards, as I was about to go to bed, there came to me, just as such things do come to one at such untimely hours, the opening idea for that entirely new work which he wanted me to write for him, and I worked at it until it was very late. A week later I had finished my score to my liking, and, as he was still in pain, I put it by and longed impatiently for the time when he would be well enough to hear it, for I knew it was good.

He was not able to think of music for yet another eight days, and when at last they had made him

comfortable in the great leather chair in the music-
room, and he had said, 'I am ready now, lad; let me
hear what you've done,' I could not contain myself,
but started off with a verve that certainly was not
English.   As I played he kept on saying, 'Good –
good – good – now more of that – yes – yes – yes,' with
eyes wide open and head shaking with interest.
'Fenby,' said he, when I had finished, 'I can work
with you. You are a natural musician. You have got
the sense of my ideas in the most wonderful way.
It seems almost uncanny. You have awakened my
interest again, and, now that you have shown me
what you can do with my material, it has set my mind
working to see what I can make of it.'

Then he said many pleasing things which will ever
remain with me.

This is how Delius began to work again after years
of inactivity. How he worked with me I will try to
explain later on.

5

I HAD now been in Grez for three weeks when the
autumn rains set in, and icy winds from Russia
stripped the leaves from the great trees by the
river till, from the music-room window, one could see
the meadows and the bleak woods beyond. There
were no more walks up the Marlotte road when all the
village had gone to bed, no more of those tusslings
with the wind, when, if you went alone, you held an
umbrella over the old man with one hand and pushed
him in his carriage with the other, with ever an
anxious eye on that miserable oil lamp, lest it should
blow out and some mad cyclist come dashing into us
in the darkness; no more of those delicious teas with
him in the garden, as we followed the sun round
greedily until it went down behind the church.
Delius loved the sun, and would often say that it was
not hard for him to understand the early Persians
worshipping it.

Each morning he would ask if the sun was out, and,
if his nurse felt energetic and told the truth, you would
hear that thunderous clearing of his throat, as they
tucked him up in his carriage down below under the
porch. I say thunderous, for I have heard it often
from the bridge a good four minutes' walk away from
the house ! Then would come that habitual question,
'Are there any letters, lass ?' and presently the sound

of his carriage bumping over the cobblestones as they wheeled him towards the garden path. Finding some sheltered spot – for a puff of wind was like a gale to him – his wife would read the mail whilst he listened with head thrown back, facing the sun, anxious lest it should quickly hide from him behind the clouds.

What questions he asked ! Had the sun gone already ? How long would it be before he could feel it again ? Was it a very big cloud, and could we move a little, so that we should face it when it came out on the other side ?

How often have I cursed that eternal game of hide-and-seek up there in the sky, when, just as I had warned him that in an instant the sun would be breaking through, some saucy wisp of a cloud would flitter by and obscure it, and the old man would complain bitterly, 'But you said it was coming – I don't feel it yet !' What excuses and what explanations there were, and what waitings that so often ended in, 'Well, never mind – wheel me round the garden and tell me how it all looks.'

On such days as he was unable to go out he used to take exercise indoors. He would try to walk. This could only be done when three of us were present – one to support him on either side and the other to follow behind him with a chair and air-cushion. I shall never forget the first time on which I assisted with the chair and cushion at these painful proceedings.

Before he could begin, his nurse carried him from his great armchair, and set him on a smaller armchair which had been devised for that particular purpose. He could not sit on a chair without arms. At a given signal he was lifted up on to his feet, and held up gently under his arms, Mrs. Delius at the one, the nurse at the other. His thinness suggested great height as they propped him up, limp and unsteady, between them, so that he towered above their stooping figures like a giant, and his clothes hung on him like a skeleton. Then Mrs. Delius coaxed him quietly: 'Are you ready, Fred? Links – rechts – links – rechts——' and so the pathetic procession began. At the word *links* he kicked out sideways with his left foot, with no sense of direction or control, and, on *rechts*, the right foot did likewise. After five or six yards of this stumping along, he cried, 'Be ready with the chair, Eric.' Then, when he was unable to totter a step farther, they lowered him gradually into it, panting for breath. When he had rested in silence for several minutes, and his breathing had become normal, we turned him about – chair and all – and he tried to walk those few paces back again.

There were many incidents at Grez that would have touched the heart of the toughest, and this was one of the most terrible of all. Yet it did me good, for I saw the iron nature and courage of the man, and I learnt in those moments how a man should bear suffering and misfortune. There was nothing of the sickly, morbid, blind composer as known by popular fiction here, but a man with a heart like a lion, and a spirit that was as untamable as it was stern.

I had not expected to find such sternness, almost harshness, in a man of his delicate susceptibility, and such uncouth passages in his work as had hitherto puzzled me now became clear. I can never listen to

the perverse insistency of those blatant chords leading
into the last movement of his Violin Concerto, when
it seems as if the whole orchestra is shaking its angry
fist at you, without being whisked off to that room in
Grez where, on more occasions than I care to remember, I have seen his expression suddenly lose its life
and set as hard as stone, for no other reason than that
the soup had not been sufficiently salted in the cook-
ing. At first, I attributed it to his illness, but on one
occasion, after it had persisted inhumanly for several
days, I broached the subject tactfully to his wife, only
to be told that I ought to have known Fred when he
was well. He was not half so hard as he had been in
those days !

This sternness was never far away from him. It
embarrassed the kindly Americans who had known
him for a lifetime in Grez – their rare visits to the
Delius household were prompted more by a sense of
obligation than of pleasure – and it terrified the children. All too frequently there were periods when
nobody came near the house for months on end, and
consequently I have gone for as long as five months
at a time without speaking to a soul outside their tiny
household.

Once you had crossed the threshold of that great
door to the street you found yourself in another world
– a world, peaceful and self-sufficient, which centred
round the figure of Delius. It was a world with its
own laws, its own standards of right and wrong in all
things, its own particular sense of beauty and its own
music. It had been created for music-making, and
there was an unheard-of reverence for work. Here

D

these two original people had lived happy and contented for many years, jealously guarding their little world from all vulgar intrusion. Within the walls of that house and garden the romance of their life together flowered and died.

No traveller, pausing on the bridge at Grez before entering the village by the lane from Moncourt, could ever imagine that over that wall between the church and the ruin there existed a world such as this. A painter's paradise, to be sure, but hardly the sort of place in which a composer would choose to spend his life. But, then, Delius had always disliked the society of musicians. He had found them such a dull and uninspiring lot, who talked about nothing else but 'technique, technique.' The world of beauty was a closed book to them, it seemed. He had much preferred the more vital companionship of painters, and Grez had always been a haunt of painters. There were old men still living who recalled how they had stood as cheeky little boys behind Corot as he worked away at his easel, puffing at his pipe under a great umbrella down by the mill.[1] Edvard Munch and Carl Larson had spent many a summer there, painting and sketching by the river, and the delightful pictures of Grez that I have seen in the art galleries of Sweden are proof of its fascination for Scandinavian artists. In particular, it is interesting to note that Carl Larson's studies of Grez in the National Museum at Stockholm are those by which he first won fame.

Writers, too, had felt something of its charm.

[1] Corot painted a beautiful picture of the old bridge at Grez, and there is an etching of it (in reverse) at the Mairie there.

Strindberg had once stayed for several weeks at the Hôtel Chevion, then a famous rendezvous for artists, and had not Robert Louis Stevenson proposed to Fanny Osbourne on the bridge ?

Once a man has come under the spell of Grez, and known all its moods, life can never be quite the same elsewhere. Like all the others, I, too, have vowed that never again would I set foot in it, yet I know that before long I shall find myself lolling on that bridge again, with my eyes turned towards that cluster of houses nestling round the church and ruin, their garden walls green with clinging vines, and quiet homeliness about their tiny wash-houses under the trees down by the water's edge, and I know that the old sense of wonder will come back to me.

Alden Brooks, Delius's friend and neighbour, who has lived in the old church house for over twenty years, once caught me in this damnatory mood. 'This wretched place is getting on my nerves,' said I. 'As for you, I cannot imagine why you go on living in this miserable swamp !'

'Oh, I have cursed it just as much as you,' replied Brooks, 'but it gets us all in the end, and we have to return. It will get you just the same, you mark my words !'

It was ever thus with Delius. He was never happy for long away from Grez.

We continued to work daily, and those days were the hardest of all for me in Grez, for we were painfully and laboriously evolving a method of work, and this was not easy. It was like groping about in the dark.

After a few weeks of this sustained effort, Delius had

managed to dictate a short work based on the good
material from *A Poem of Life and Love*, and this score
was sent to Balfour Gardiner for his inspection. The
latter had been very sceptical about the possibility of
Delius's working any more. 'For one thing,' he had
said to me, 'Fred will never be able to dictate because
of his inability to make a decision.' Balfour Gardiner
was almost right here, for Delius's constant change-
ableness was the most difficult thing with which I had
to contend. Delius was very pleased with his achievement, and wondered what his friend would have to
say. He had already composed some of the incidental
music to Flecker's *Hassan* by dictation to his wife, but
he was then still able to see, and could therefore correct
the score, even though he could not do it with his own
hand. Percy Grainger had also very kindly helped
him with the scoring. Now it was a different matter.
Delius had to picture each page of the score in his
mind, and work it out in his head, away from the
piano, before he could dictate it. He had not been
accustomed to doing this, so that now there were
greater demands on his memory, not to mention the
ticklish problem of picking up the threads of a previous
day's work, and continuing, logically and fittingly, in
accordance with what he wanted to express. This he
found a very trying and troublesome stumbling-block.

Several days later, Balfour Gardiner wrote to Mrs.
Delius saying, 'When I opened the parcel containing
the score, I was astonished at what I found. I thought
there would be numerous sketches all pieced together,
with some parts scored and others not, and a great
mass of material for me to deal with. Instead, I find

a short work practically completed and ready for the copyist. All that remains for me to do is to go over the score in detail and suggest minor improvements.'

Shortly afterwards, I received a long letter from him full of helpful and constructive criticism. It ended:

'You have certainly achieved the object you set out to achieve, namely, making a coherent musical whole out of the elements at your disposal, and the solution of the problems involved must have been of the greatest interest both to Fred and yourself. If any remarks I have made lead to improvements, even small improvements in detail, I shall have been amply repaid for my trouble. . . .'

This kindly and practical interest was greatly appreciated by Delius, and, I may add, by myself, and, coming as it did at the right moment from a musician of whom Delius thought so highly, was the very best possible incentive to renew his efforts, in the hope that something worth while might eventually be accomplished. But there was much to be done yet. It was not until six months later that Delius began to dictate with anything approaching confidence and certainty, and I to take it down with anything like the understanding and quick anticipation that was necessary.

That Christmas, Evlyn and Grace Howard-Jones came over from London, and there was much music-making and laughter, and Delius called for champagne at the slightest provocation. The children's party on Christmas Eve, which Delius had stipulated was to last no more than one hour, was a moderate success.

I had had a shock earlier in the day that set me thinking hard, when I had discovered that one of the children who had come to prepare the crib was putting twins into the manger ! So much for the compulsory State education of modern France ! The electric lights were turned out, the Christmas-tree and crib now blazed with candles, and there were carols on the gramophone. Each child received a present, and I, being one of them, found that my parcel contained a vocal score of *A Village Romeo and Juliet.*

Then what was to have been a surprise turned out a miserable failure. Up on the landing Howard-Jones, the maid Hildegarde, and I waited to sing a little three-part carol that I had written as a boy:

> Behold a silly, tender Babe,
> In freezing winter night,
> In homely manger trembling lies;
> Alas ! a piteous sight.
>
> The inns are full, no man will yield
> This little Pilgrim bed;
> But forced He is with silly beasts
> In crib to shroud His Head.

Our days of practising had been in vain, for at the crucial moment the male voices were heard, but from our little Hildegarde there came not a sound. Her lips moved, but still she was silent. We struggled on as best we could, the pair of us, to finish the verse, and had no sooner ended this than her voice returned. But, instead of trying to patch up my ruined carol, she began another, and this at the top of her voice – 'Holy Night, Silent Night,' her annual effort, and the one thing she had been forbidden to sing. After the

seventh verse Delius sent up to say that he could bear
it no longer. Could we possibly silence her ? We
were just in time to prevent her starting the eighth by
applauding vigorously. She then retired to the
kitchen and wept bitterly.

All through these proceedings, Delius had sat in the
middle of the room, deathly white, silent and aloof,
framed off from the rest by a screen round the back
of his chair. As each child, painfully nervous and
with fear in its eyes, was brought forward and intro-
duced to him, he smiled, but there was nothing of that
easy manner that a child instinctively looks for, and
which wins its affection from the very first. His
attempts at conversation were awkward, strained, and
hollow, so that the children withdrew as soon as they
could and stood about the room in silence.

Even admitting his blindness, and the embarrass-
ment which his infirmities caused him, one would
have thought that a man who had written such tender
music as so often smiles through the pages of his
works would not have been so ill at ease with children.

6

I FOUND the intense cold of that winter[1] unbearable, but there was some small consolation on hearing Delius say that it was the worst winter that he had ever known in Grez. For several weeks we had been snowbound, and I had rarely left the house except to trudge down the garden to admire the magnificent line of silver birches all glittering in the moonlight in his meadow on the opposite bank of the river. I revelled in its glassy stillness and the inky drawing of the trees in the woods near by. Then when the thaw came, and there was no snow to temper the biting cold, it seemed that we had touched one of the fierce extremes of Dante's Inferno.

There was no central heating in the house in those days, nor were there open fires, and in my wing I had to rely on a comfortless stove that stood cheerless as a pillar-box at the end of the music-room. My bedroom was the coldest room in the house, and night after night I could not sleep for the penetrating cold. For nearly a fortnight now the water in my room had been frozen inches thick. My hair-brushes were like bricks, my shaving-brush like a piece of wood. I was obliged to chisel up my soap, and the hot water which they sent me from the kitchen was tepid when it

[1] 1928–9.

reached me. I thawed my things as best I could, but before I could use them they were stiff again.

Men in these parts mind not how they dress, caring more for comfort than for fashion, and during these icy days those who were obliged to go out of doors paid no heed to their appearance. A more comical set of rogues I never saw, as they clattered hurriedly through the streets in their sabots, with coarse mufflers lashed about the pointed hoods of their black capes. Some had sacks tied round them with rope, and all were reluctant to greet you, lest they should bare their faces for an instant to the cold.

During those icy days work with Delius was impossible, yet he was by no means idle, for that crude and gallant attempt at composition had stirred him deeply. He had told his wife that it would need patience – great patience – both on his and my part, if ultimately he was to write something worthy of performance. It was no use our tackling works that he had in mind until we had created and mastered a technique by which we could work, and that would take time – perhaps a very long time. The only way was to learn by doing, otherwise we could never hope to understand each other. We must treat this piece as an exercise, and, guided by Balfour Gardiner's helpful criticism, hammer away at it until we could knock it into shape.

'I cannot tell you,' said Mrs. Delius, one morning when she had brought up my letters to the music-room, 'I cannot tell you what it means to me to see Fred full of his music again. Twice he has asked me not to read to him at the customary times; he would prefer to think of his work. When I awoke this morning he was already deep in thought, and humming some of the music from that piece that you are working on together. I did not stir, but after a while he suddenly called out, "Jelka, Jelka, write to Universal for the score of *Hassan*. I have been thinking in the night that I could make a choral suite out of it." '

His interest was gradually reviving.

When we resumed work, I soon saw that he had not suffered the grass to grow under his feet, and there were fierce discussions when he suggested that we should retain some of the rejected material from the old score, *A Poem of Life and Love*. Still, it said a great deal for his open-mindedness that he had been willing to sacrifice so much of it in the beginning; therefore I kept my place and let him have his own way. His mind was working so quickly that it was always ahead of what he was dictating, but I noted that he put his finger immediately on the weak spots of such small sections as hung fire, and quickly brought them to life.

And so we grappled with our problem, and Delius grew stronger, until one day, on awakening out of his usual nap after lunch, he astonished his wife by crying out excitedly, 'Jelka, I can see my hands !' Scarcely had he uttered these startling words than the vision faded.

This hopeful sign recurred fairly frequently within the next few months, though never for more than a few moments each time, and high hopes were entertained that by the end of the year he might see again. The tissues of his eyes were sound and healthy, they

told me, and if, in some mysterious way, strength
could be infused into him, he would see. It was not
that he experienced merely a momentary perception
of light; he told me that he could 'see well enough to
count his fingers.'

It was all a mystery to me, and I let it remain so.

Try as I would, I could not convince myself that
Delius would eventually see, though I somehow
managed to mask my true feelings under a conventional cheerfulness that was not always easy to sustain.
It seemed against all natural laws that this man would
ever be anything other than the hopeless wreck he was.
The amazing thing was that he was still so mentally
alive. His conversation was never heavy; on the
contrary, and in spite of his slowness of speech, there
was something about it that smacked of Latin gaiety.

I noticed that as time went on he became increasingly talkative over lunch, and would comment on
the contents of the daily newspaper in a mocking tone
which I should have hated in others, yet in him was
wholly delicious. He would switch from one topic to
another with a swiftness that was as bewildering as it
was often embarrassing.

I remember one instance on the occasion of a visit
from Suzanne Haym, the youngest daughter of Dr.
Hans Haym, whom both Delius and his wife had not
met since she was a tiny tot at the production of
Koanga at Elberfeld in 1904. Delius had been telling
us that he had had a letter that morning from a man
who, confusing him with a certain Delius living in
Harrogate, had written, 'I wonder if you are that
Delius whom I knew at school fifty years ago; he was

great on the trombone and I was great on the jews'
harp, and they used to call me "Fiddle-Face." '

Instantly, and with little change in his voice, he
went on, 'Suzanne, we'll drink to the memory of your
father. It was through his efforts that my music first
became known in Germany. I owe him a tremendous
lot for what he did for me in those days.'

Dr. Haym had died of a broken heart after losing
two sons in the war.

Already I was beginning to feel the strain of going
from day to day and hearing little or nothing else but
Delius's music.

It was easy to understand that, when either Delius
or his wife desired music, they should choose the
music that had been most intimately bound up with
their own lives. We all do this when the mood is upon
us. They were both at a seasoned age when they
were living in the past, whereas I was a raw young
man who had barely begun to live. With them it was
always the music of Delius. With me it was not quite
so simple.

Years before I had heard of the existence of Delius,
my deepest feelings had found utterance in the finest
music of Palestrina, Victoria, Mozart and Elgar.
Now, starved as I was of all young society – indeed,
any society other than that of these two old people –
with only the sweet and luscious wine of Delius's
music to live on (for that which had once been a
delectable dessert had now become my staple food),
there was a risk lest my musical digestion should be
ruined for ever. Music is as necessary for my well-being

as food and wine. I cannot go for long without it. Yet no man can live on champagne for ever.

A musical friend of Delius, who had spent weeks correcting the proofs of *Sea-drift*, once told me, in the presence of the composer's wife, that in consequence he could not bear to hear that work again. From now onwards I, too, began to feel something of that same feeling with every score that we worked on. Norman O'Neill was also fully aware of this danger, for I remember his saying to me, 'Fenby, when you leave Grez, you will never want to hear another note of Delius as long as you live!'

It would have been so refreshing if, after a hard day's work, one could have listened for a while to music that was just a little less chromatic in character. But, when there was to be music, it was always the same few records that we heard—*On Hearing the First Cuckoo in Spring, Summer Night on the River, Summer Garden, Brigg Fair*, or *The Walk to the Paradise Garden*. Many a time after these recitals I have gone up to the music-room at night and played the opening bars of Sibelius's Second Symphony over and over again, but Sibelius would have frowned had he heard the number of times I repeated that strong opening chord of D major before moving away from it!

Perhaps twice during the course of a week Delius would 'listen in' to a Strauss waltz, or some rare and seldom-heard piece by Grieg that he had told them to mark when they had read through the programmes of the *World Radio* to him; but even here I always felt that his interest was prompted more by the recollection of some pleasing incident associated with the performance of this or that particular work in the past than by any purely musical desire to hear it again.

However, he seldom missed an opportunity of listening in to a new work, but it was not long before he would ask us to turn it off and go on with the reading.

Sometimes, after he had been carried up to bed, I would play the rebel boy and 'tune in' some favourite work of mine that chanced to be broadcast. Then, suddenly, I would hear that loud clearing of his throat as if he were yet in the room, and, stealing on tiptoe up the staircase, I would discover that he had ordered his bedroom door to be opened – but just a little !

The next morning it was invariably the same question that he put to me as soon as I had entered the room:

'Did you like that music that you were listening to last night ?'

'Yes.'

'Well, I didn't !'

7

IN the early days of March the icy wind suddenly
left us, the air was mild and soft again, and the
lower and wilder part of the garden pale and beautiful with shy flowers. The old peasant woman with
the home-made, home-cured rabbit-skin coat now put
it away, hoping that before another winter set in she
would have a few more pieces to sew on to keep her
from the cold. The merry widow at the little inn
opposite bustled about in preparation for Easter, and
the postman lingered a little less in the warmth by
the way. Now we were able to take tea in the garden
almost every day.

Hitherto Delius had rarely left the house except
to sit in the open facing the garden in the shelter of
the porch to the main door. On one of these rare
occasions I was sitting beside him, reading aloud,
when there came a knock on the door.

'Eric, would you mind answering it ?' said he. 'The
servants are busy down the garden, I believe.'

I opened the tiny door within the *porte-cochère*, and
a strange young man greeted me in English:

'Excuse me, sir. I am a reporter from the British
United Press in Paris. May I speak to Mr. Delius ?'

Before I could say a word, from out the mass of
top-coats, rugs, mufflers, and screens not two yards
away came a loud and angry voice, 'I can't see him.

Tell him I'm out !' Whereupon the young man, greatly astonished, bowed and quickly walked away.

Earlier in the year Sir Thomas Beecham had given a Delius concert to a private audience at Kingsway Hall, and this, happily for us, was broadcast. The programme, much to Delius's delight, included *Paris* and two works which were greatly neglected in those days – Dance Rhapsody No. 2 and *Eventyr*, a ballad for orchestra inspired by the 'once upon a time' of Norwegian folk-lore.

Delius was very amused by Sir Thomas's remarks before conducting the Dance Rhapsody. In words something like these we heard him say, 'Ladies and gentlemen, the next piece we are going to play is the least known of Delius's orchestral works – his second Dance Rhapsody. This is not strange, for, though this unfortunate work has been given on several occasions, it has not yet been heard at all ! You will now hear the first performance !'

He then gave a thrilling interpretation, and Delius, in his usual manner of addressing the conductor as if he were in the room, said, 'Perfect, Thomas; perfect !' Each work brought forth comment such as this, and by the end of the programme his enthusiasm knew no bounds.

'I should be content with a few superlative performances like these each year,' he afterwards confided, 'rather than the mediocre ones that I all too frequently hear.'

As he himself was unable to do so, Delius usually insisted on my following broadcast performances of his music with the full scores. His criticisms were often scathing. More than once I have heard him exclaim, 'Whatever should I do without Beecham !'

In the light of what followed, it seemed to us that this concert had been something in the nature of an experiment, for now Sir Thomas wrote to say that he intended organising a festival of Delius's music, which he hoped would take place that autumn.

Delius merely wagged his head and said that it sounded 'too good to be true.'

Flying visits from Barjansky and Balfour Gardiner broke the monotony of our weeks of loneliness. The latter, especially, was most encouraging, and suggested schemes for making various *Hassan* suites. All these projects came to nothing in the end, but they provided me with a great deal of experience and work, which I found invaluable later on.

Shortly after Easter we had three more visitors – Roger Quilter, of whom Delius was particularly fond, Dr. Simon, then editor of the *Frankfurter Zeitung* and an old and valued friend, and Professor Dent, who was busy working on his study of Busoni, and had come to talk to Delius about their mutual friend.

I remember that it struck me as very strange that Delius had so little to say about Busoni, but a great deal about old Ferdinando, Gerda, and Benni. Later in the day, when the professor had gone, Delius told me how much he had admired Busoni when first they had met, but, almost in spite of himself, he had had to admit that Busoni had never acted quite fairly with him. He had promised to play Delius's Pianoforte Concerto – that is, the first version – but when the time had come, and Delius had left his work at Grez and gone purposely to Berlin at Busoni's invitation to hear it, Busoni had made excuses at the last moment and withdrawn it from the programme. There had not been time to prepare it properly; he would play it at his next concert. But, somehow or other, it was always the same tale, and so poor Delius had wasted a whole winter's work hanging about Berlin in miserable uncertainty, and this at a stage when he had very little money, and when the performance of his music by the already established Busoni would have meant everything to him.

When eventually Busoni had tried to make amends by conducting the first performance of *Paris* at his second concert of new music at the Beethoven-Saal in November of 1902, Delius complained that 'Busoni did not know the score,' and that 'the work went so badly, I could hardly recognise my own music !'

According to his wife, Delius turned deathly pale during the performance, and made no comment when the music ceased. The next day they left for Grez and home.

There was always this to be said for Delius: that no matter how much they maltreated his music – and, judging by what he has told me at various times, he must have endured some ghastly performances in his day – his belief in himself and his work was unshakable.

Interesting as all these visitors were, I burned with curiosity to meet that young man who had done so much for Delius since he was little more than a schoolboy – Philip Heseltine. Delius had made scant reference to him when I had enquired about him, and I gathered that there had been some slight estrangement between them, so I had dropped the subject.

Imagine my surprise when, one morning, on going down to lunch, I discovered that Heseltine and several other people had arrived unexpectedly. They were not at their full strength, they told us, for they had missed 'Old Raspberry'[1] on the way; he would probably be coming along later in the day !

Delius, extremely sensitive at all times to his physical disabilities, and pathetically so in the presence of strangers, was furious, and refused to see Philip. Why had he brought this crowd of people with him ? Finally, after some gentle persuasion on the part of his wife, Delius agreed to be carried downstairs, and so the whole party stayed to lunch. Conversation was not easy, for the others, excepting Anthony Bernard, appeared to be entirely unmusical, and it was natural that we should want to talk about music. There were, however, occasional flashes of brilliant observation from Heseltine. I envied him his splendid command of words, and liked the way he looked you full in the eye whilst addressing you. Few people do this. I shall never forget him for it.

I could see that Delius was still ruffled and not at his ease, and I was relieved when they had taken him away to rest, and I was sauntering down the garden path with Heseltine, leaving Mrs. Delius to amuse his friends. We chatted affably enough, but by the time we had reached the pond I found myself wondering whether this could possibly be the same Heseltine

[1] The identity of this musician must remain a mystery.

who had written that glowing book about Delius and his work, for whenever there was an opening to attack the music he had once championed, he thrust his critical rapier in, hilt and all.   I knew nothing at the time of the reactionary phase through which Heseltine was then passing in respect of Delius's music, and it astonished me greatly to hear him say that out of Delius's enormous output, three of the major works only would live – *Sea-drift*, *A Village Romeo and Juliet*, and *Appalachia*.   Whether he persisted in this attitude to the end, I do not know.

It must not be imagined that I have been a blind admirer of Delius's music, but I was not prepared to dismiss all save a handful of works as entirely worthless.   I agreed with him that *Sea-drift* and *A Village Romeo and Juliet* were great masterpieces, but I would not have placed *Appalachia* in their company; nor could I understand his enthusiasm for a comparatively poor piece like the Air and Dance for strings.

(I remember how, after the performance of *Appalachia* at the Delius Festival later that year, we were coming down in the lift together at the Langham Hotel, after having escorted Delius safely across from Queen's Hall, and Heseltine saying, 'Well, Fenby, what do you think of it now ?   Wasn't it magnificent ? It's a superb work !'

'I'm sorry,' I replied, 'but I still think the opening is slovenly, and, if I may say so, the whole work much too long. The amazing thing to my mind is that some of the best variations are as fine as they are, when one considers the rather silly tune on which they are built.')

Appalachia has never been a particular favourite of mine.

From Delius he turned to van Dieren, for whom, both as composer and man, he had the warmest admiration. Did I know his music, and had I heard the last quartet which van Dieren had dedicated to him ? He would send me a score, for it was a 'superlatively fine work.' Had Fred heard Bartók's Quartet (No. 4) the other night on the wireless ?

Now it happened that just at that moment we were about to enter the living-room again; Delius had already been brought down from his nap, and was holding forth to Bernard about some work being 'infantile and horrible.'

'What is that, Fred, that you are talking about ?' asked Heseltine.

'Oh, Bartók's Fourth Quartet,' replied Delius. 'Did you hear it, Phil ?'

'Yes.'

'So did I. I thought it was dreadful ! I'm sick and tired to death of all this laboured writing, all this unnecessary complication, these harsh, brutal, and uncouth noises. How anybody çan listen to such excruciating sounds with understanding and pleasure is beyond me ! What did you think of it, Phil ?'

'I'm sorry, Fred, but I don't agree with you. I think it's a masterpiece. For sheer beauty of sound it is one of the wonders of music.'

'Well,' sighed Delius, shaking his head, 'well ! . . .' and relapsed into silence.

After tea Heseltine asked me to take him up to the music-room. He could not believe that 'old Fred'

(Delius) was trying to work again, and when he saw what had been done he exclaimed, 'My God, how you both must have slaved at this !'

It was now getting dark, so he proposed that the party should leave, and walk over to Marlotte to see his Uncle Joe (Joe Heseltine). 'No visit to Europe is complete,' said he, 'unless one has seen old Joe's pictures.' In fact, there was one masterpiece, showing a horse and cart coming down a road, but the proportions of the cart had somehow got so much out of hand that he had been obliged to sew another lump of canvas on, higher up the road, to get the cart in ! Old Fred and old Joe had not been on very friendly terms since the war, for old Joe had gone about telling everybody that Delius was a German spy, and that the strategic point of the whole world war was centred on the bridge at Grez. It had been a blind, Delius's living there all these years. He had been posted there by the Germans, and they knew what they were about. Every night he was up there in the church tower signalling to the enemy. Feeling in the village had become so hostile that on one occasion they had broken Fred's windows.

I saw very little of old Joe – once when he was sitting asleep at a local sale, under a white-hot sun, amid the shouts of the bidders and the crashes of the hammer, and now and then strolling about the streets of Fontainebleau. He used to come over from Marlotte to see Delius on an old tricycle fitted up with all manner of gadgets and accessories – his painting outfit, his waterproof, his kettle, and a complete change of clothes. Having knocked at the great door and been admitted, he would take no notice of anyone, but calmly wheel his machine into the courtyard, and then, retiring behind the pergola, would change his entire outfit. Not until he emerged did the visit begin.

Our rowdy friends had not been gone more than a few minutes when 'Old Raspberry' drove up in a taxi; but we pushed him in again and directed the driver to Marlotte. Delius had had enough for one day.

Within a fortnight Philip Heseltine was back again, discussing the coming festival and acting as a link between the composer and Sir Thomas Beecham. This time he came alone, and stayed at a little inn kept by an Italian hard by the canal at Moncourt, the tiny hamlet I have already mentioned, which is reached by taking the lane over the bridge at Grez and continuing along it until one has crossed the canal.

Two or three days before this second visit I had started to read Cecil Gray's *History of Music* to Delius, but the old man, much to my annoyance, had insisted on skipping the chapter on Gregorian chant. This did not deter me from reading it for myself, and I was glad that I did so, for I thought it the best essay I had ever read on that fascinating subject. I was therefore full of it when Heseltine came, and was not surprised to find that he, too, agreed with me. The discovery that I knew and admired so much of that older and satisfying music that was so dear to his heart delighted him, and we ferreted about in our minds for the names of such old motets, masses, and madrigals as contained some delicious harmonic touch or daring modulation as had never failed to captivate us. He had been luckier than I, for he had heard them in actual performance, whereas I had merely read them or played them at the keyboard. In Sir Richard Terry's time, he told me, he had been continually in and out of Westminster Cathedral. The music in those days had been worth hearing. He deplored the general apathy of the Catholic clergy to the glorious music of the Church. It was a pity that priests were so seldom musical, and, when they were musically inclined, they were usually amateurs of the worst type. I, too, had often remarked that, contrary to common belief, monks, nuns, and priests were usually quite unmusical, and that a religious temperament rarely went hand in hand with a musical feeling.

At this moment Delius's carriage came into sight round the bend by the bamboos, and, mindful of the fact that Delius had about as much use for monks, nuns, and priests as he had for that older music, I winked at Heseltine, who, having said that for years he had had no patience with Fred's eternal tiltings at Christianity, began a very knowledgeable discourse on the decline of English beer.

That night after supper Heseltine suggested that I should walk back to Moncourt and sit and drink with him. When I hesitated, he looked at me appealingly and said, 'For God's sake, Fenby, do come, I cannot bear to be alone ! Bring the miniature score of Fred's Quartet; I haven't seen it for ages, and we'll read it together.'

As we crossed the ugly modern bridge at Moncourt,

we idled a little by the railings, peering down into
the hold of a neat and brightly painted barge, which
they had been loading with white sand. A great
Alsatian looked up at us as it sprawled beside the
mast, and, seeing that we meant no harm, buried its
head in its paws. Some men were smoking and
drinking at a little table under an enormous poplar
which stood in stately solitude outside the *buvette* at
the corner of the street. They took no notice of us
as we passed by, nor did the two barge mules that
were grazing contentedly on the little common, and
as we walked on by the edge of the canal the golden
rim of the setting sun disappeared behind the trees
at the other side of the water, and all was peace.

We entered the inn, and Heseltine called for red
wine. We had not gone far with our reading of the
Quartet when the door opened and Alden Brooks and
Matthew Smith came in, but, observing that we were
immersed in some musical discussion, they left us
alone to it, and did not join us until Heseltine,
suddenly exasperated, threw the score down on the
table in utter disgust and declared in a loud voice that
Fred could not write for strings. If only he had half
of Elgar's cunning in this respect! Give him his
way, and he would make every student buy the score
of Elgar's Introduction and Allegro for Strings, for
he considered it to be the finest piece of writing for
strings in the whole literature of music. He got up
excitedly and paced about the room, and Brooks
chaffed him, and Smith eyed him whimsically through
his large spectacles, and said nothing.

And when we had settled all the questions of the

day, and had drunk far more than was good for us, we remembered that even artists must sometimes go to bed. Had we known how little we were to see Heseltine again before his tragic death, there would have been no inclination to go to bed that night at all. I was sorry when he left for London the next evening, and for the first time since my arrival in Grez I felt homesick. But I had become so attached to Delius and his wife that I could not leave them, for had not they just told me that I had supplied a want in their simple life so perfectly that they could not now imagine it without me ?

They had always thought it unaccountable that I had suddenly come, like a bolt out of the blue, and adapted myself to their needs, yet I knew that the secret of our happy relationship was simply this – that I always knew when to keep quiet. There were evenings when I had pushed the old man up the Marlotte road in his carriage, and from leaving the house to returning to it, over an hour later, there had never been a word spoken between us. 'Thank you, lad, that was grand !' he would say as I afterwards left him when they had come to carry him up to bed.

I have always been a great lover of dogs, and by this time I had made friends with most of the dogs of the village, so that now I rarely went out alone. One night, on one of these silent walks, we collected no less than five of my friends as we passed along the village street. They accompanied us slowly and silently up the road, turning when we turned, with never a bark, not even at one another, and so completely were they in tune with our mood that Delius never knew they were there.

Sometimes we varied this evening procedure by going on the river. Delius used to sit in a deck-chair propped up with cushions, in the wide, flat-bottomed boat which was always anchored ready for use among the water-lilies in a tiny inlet beneath the mighty trees that stretched far out over the river, sheltering the fishermen from the fierce heat of the sun as they dozed over their rods. In the cool of the evening I loved nothing better than to take the oars and row the old man and his wife up as far as *le bout du monde*, and, turning, let the boat drift back with the current. And when with difficulty we had landed our frail and precious burden, and were wheeling him up to the house, through the garden fragrant with the delicious scent of lilac and apple-blossom under the blue and cloudless sky, it seemed that of all young musicians I was the most highly favoured to be here, and in my contentment my loneliness left me.

8

I HAD been looking through a great pile of pencilled sketches of all manner of works that Delius had made before I was born and, coming upon a particularly faded manuscript, I racked my brain to place it in the list of his published works. I could not remember it at all, and yet, at the entry of the voice, there was a tiny figure in the wood-wind that instantly brought to mind *Songs of Sunset*.

I was on the point of dismissing it as nothing more than some rejected sketch, for Delius often turned back to his very early work and extracted a lovely bar here and sometimes a fine passage there (for instance, one of those fine soaring passages in the 'Cello Sonata appears almost note for note in an early romance for 'cello and piano; the germ of that beautiful and romantic melody in *Paris* which steals in on the violas is to be found in an early tone poem for orchestra called *Hiawatha*. Delius's music teems with examples of this habit. In fact, in a much more subtle and less obvious degree, the score of *A Village Romeo and Juliet* contains the germs of all the music that was to come after it, and is a happy hunting-ground for people who have time for this sport). I was on the point of dismissing it, I say, when it occurred to me that it would be fun to play it over. This was not easy, for, after the first page, there were no indications

in the wood-wind and brass as to what instruments
these faintly pencilled notes and phrases were to be
given, and at first sight I could only surmise, by their
vague positions on the score-paper, that such and such
a phrase looked like a bassoon counterpoint, and some
such other looked like an English-horn part. Gradually I got the hang of the thing as far as it went, for it
was unfinished, but the supper-bell rang out from the
porch before I could place the words. I did not know
Dowson's poem at the time, and when I went down
to supper I asked Delius if he remembered making a
rough draft of a work for baritone and orchestra, in
which he had used that little four-note figure that
haunts the pages of *Songs of Sunset*:

To which he replied that he did not, but that if I
would play it over to him that night he might be able
to enlighten me.

When they had taken him up to bed and had opened
the doors to the music-room, the gods lent me their
fingers and their eyes, and one of them even held the
great score-paper up, such a fumbler am I when it
comes to turning over ! Yet they never came to help
me in my boyhood, when, alone in the organ-loft, I
have struggled with some puck of a page that had the
very devil in it – but why bring that in here ? My
organ days are done.

Yes, he remembered it now. It was a sketch for a
setting of Dowson's 'Cynara.' He had written it
twenty-four years before, intending to include it as

one of the numbers in *Songs of Sunset* which he was then composing. But he had found that, like old Joe Heseltine's cart, it did not quite fit into the picture, so he had left it unfinished, and had never given it a thought since.

Before saying good night, I read through the poem to him, and several days later he was carried up to the music-room and, as I recollect only too well, began to work on the score again with an excitement that puzzled me.

The completed score was sent to Philip Heseltine (who knew of its existence in sketch form), who wrote to Delius saying that he was delighted with the beautiful way in which the composer had been able to finish it. *Cynara* received its first performance at the Delius Festival four months later. It is not one of Delius's happiest inspirations, but there was a moment in the green-room at Queen's Hall when, suddenly coming in from the noise of the street, I heard the distant sounds of its quietly ascending introduction for divided strings as it was being rehearsed, and there seemed to be no fairer music in the world than this. But, then, I was starved. I had not heard the sound of the orchestra in the concert-room for over a year.

Another work which I unearthed for the festival was a setting for tenor voice and orchestra of Henley's poem, 'The Late Lark.' This had been misplaced, though not forgotten, and the old man had been most anxious that I should turn the place upside down, if need be, to find it, for he had a rare affection for it, and, once it was found, was continually asking me to play it over to him. Together with *A Poem of Life and Love*, he had sketched it out just before his sight had failed him. There were one or two minor adjustments to be made before it finally satisfied him, and several lines in the voice part which had yet to be filled in; this he did by dictation.

I wonder what Donizetti or old Rossini would have had to say about this tame, contemptuous afterthought of a vocal line? Probably something quite as unprintable as Delius's opinion of the poverty-stricken accompaniments which they had written to their immortal arias! Still, I knew that of the two evils I preferred the – dare I say it? – more musical and instrumental style of the Italians in writing for the voice. Enough has been said about both schools, but for me there is no more to be said of the poetry, sunny grace, the easy, effortless, cast-away-care rhapsody of that spontaneous thing of beauty, a lovely Italian aria, than that it is pure music, just pure music. A third-rate Rossini is more bearable than a second-rate Wolf, but Wolf is – well, what can one say of a song like 'Wer sich der Einsamkeit ergibt,' that brings the tears to one's eyes with its opening chords, or of an aria like 'Una voce poco fa qui nel cor,' except that we should be truly grateful for them both, worlds apart though they be? Delius, in writing for the voice, had neither feeling for line nor feeling for words. Awkward in these things though he was, he was never careless. As with *Cynara*, I was astonished to find that he took more pains with what he considered to be the correct declamation of Henley's words than he did with the shape of the melodic line to which they were to be sung.

Once, when I had read the poem through to him —

A late lark twitters from the quiet skies;
And from the west,
Where the sun, his day's work ended,
Lingers as in content,
There falls on the old, grey city
An influence luminous and serene,
A shining peace.

The smoke ascends
In a rosy-and-golden haze. The spires
Shine, and are changed. In the valley
Shadows rise. The lark sings on. The sun,
Closing his benediction,
Sinks, and the darkening air
Thrills with the sense of the triumphing night —
Night with her train of stars
And her great gift of sleep.

So be my passing !
My task accomplished and the long day done,
My wages taken, and in my heart
Some late lark singing,
Let me be gathered to the quiet west,
The sundown splendid and serene,
Death —

and had finished playing his setting of it, he said, 'Yes, that is how I want to go.'

Though he had often seemed so near to death, and had so often startled me by looking its very image, as he sat propped up in his chair listening to our reading, he had never referred to it before save once, and this rather mockingly. In his youth he had been nearly shipwrecked off the coast of Norway, and, when all had seemed lost, a parson, in his bunk below, had annoyed him so much by his long and lugubrious praying aloud that Delius had called out to him, 'Look here, my friend, just make less row. You can't be so keen to go to that heaven of yours if you're so anxious to be saved !'

Having related this incident, he added thoughtfully, 'So long as I can enjoy the taste of my food and drink, and hear the sound of my music, I want to live. Not being able to see does not trouble me. I have my imagination. Besides, I have seen the best of the earth and done everything that is worth doing; I am content. I have had a wonderful life.'

Death, when it did come to him, was indeed terrible.

9

Pᴇʀᴄʏ Gʀᴀɪɴɢᴇʀ had been a great favourite of
Delius from the day they had met, when Grainger
was a fascinating young fellow, full of original
ideas, with the energy of a team of men and the looks
of an Apollo. They had seen a great deal of each
other in those pre-war days of which I and the rest
of my generation can hope to know nothing; happy
days in England, when Delius was still well, and in
Germany, when he could still see and was yet able to
shuffle along by the help of a supporting arm. Latterly
Grainger had visited Delius at his tiny house up in
the wilds of Norway, and to the Herculean efforts of
his young friend he owed one of the sights of his
lifetime, and this just before it was too late. Delius,
with something of that same restlessness that had
animated his youth when, the moment work was
done, he would rush off for a long walk, or a long
cycle-ride, or a strenuous holiday climbing the
mountains in his beloved Norway, and anxious to
add another leaf to that inner book on which he was
soon solely to rely, had insisted on being carried up a
high mountain close by, to watch the marvellous
sunset on the great hills in the distance. Grainger
at one end, and Mrs. Delius and two servants at the
other, had borne the brunt of that seven hours'
ascent, lugging him up the mountain track in an

improvised chair on poles. As they had neared the
summit all had seemed in vain, for enormous clouds
now piled themselves up as if to spite the very mountains their grandeur, so jealously did they hide the
sun from view. But at the great moment, 'knowing
that Nature never did betray the heart that loved her,'
not even so far as to deny this singer a last sight of the
high hills whose song he had sung, the clouds dis-
persed at her bidding, and the dreamer revelled in his
sunset. Within a few minutes a dense mist had settled
over the scene, and the party began the perilous
descent.

   .   .   .   .

And now Grainger announced his intention of spending a fortnight in Grez that June (1929). Delius was
delighted. A few days before his arrival I received a
parcel of arrangements of his music, 'dished up' for one
or two pianos, with a note saying that he would like to
play them over with me to Fred. Amongst these were
'The Arrival Platform Humlet' – the sort of thing one
was expected to whistle whilst awaiting the arrival of
one's girl at the station – 'The Drunken Sailor,' 'The
Stable-boy's Romance,' several 'Room-music Tit-
Bits,' his 'Hill-Song,' and an excellent MS. arrangement for two pianos of Delius's *Song of the High Hills*.
There were 'many more to follow,' and some 'choral
and piano-scores (to sing from),' but these we did not
need. All these arrangements, with their curious
directions – 'louden slightly,' 'louden lots,' 'accom-
panyingly,' 'very rhythmicly but not unclingingly' –
were obviously the work of a first-rate musician,
certainly of a very unusual person.

It was a sweltering day, with scarcely a breath of air, and the gardener was in hiding down the garden with his bottle of red wine, when Grainger and his wife, a sturdy and good-looking Scandinavian with soft eyes, walked into the courtyard below. To our astonishment, Grainger said that he felt cold, and shortly afterwards appeared wearing thick breeches with puttees, a heavy shirt, and an enormous sweater. He must have been nearer fifty than forty, but he looked not a day older than thirty. He had a fine, arresting, yet rather boyish head, and I liked the look in his eyes. But for his fair bushy hair, one would have thought that here was a professional athlete. He was smaller than I had expected him to be, and moved with all the alacrity of a man very wide awake.

The more vigorous sports have never been in my line, but that fortnight I did more chasing about than in all my schooldays put together. Up with the blacksmith in the morning, Grainger used to drag me out of bed to go running with him. Now, I should not have minded a gentle trot before breakfast each morning, but when you were expected to gallop along and catch a ring that was being thrown at you like lightning from all angles, to fling it back with equal zest, and to keep up this strenuous performance for as long as you were able, I regretted that I had misspent my sports days idling with a book whilst my more active schoolfellows showed off their prowess before adoring females. This galloping about was not confined to out of doors. Grainger would dash from one room to another, and, bounding down the staircase in two jumps, fly through the doorway in mid-air and land with a crash beside Delius's carriage half-way across the yard; the old man would shake his head and say that he really could not bear it.

Once when we had gone round to see Brooks, and were sitting on the terrace overlooking his garden, somebody made a remark about an amazing jump he had witnessed; in fact, it was almost as high as the terrace.

'Why, that's nothing,' said Grainger, and, before we could say a word, he had sprung up from his seat, cleared the parapet, and disappeared from sight !

'Thank God there isn't a greenhouse down there,' said I to Brooks, who was still sitting speechless in his chair. A few seconds later Grainger came running up the steps from the garden, and would have jumped over again had we not forcibly dissuaded him. I had noticed that if he accompanied us on our evening walks, he never left the house with us in the normal way, but always sprang into our midst from a window facing the street. Brooks now began to dare him to do this, that, and the other, but Grainger could do everything. And when they had said that there was one thing he could not do, namely, to stand on the terrace below the house and from there throw a tennis-ball over the house, then run up the dozen steps to the door, through the house, and catch it before it fell into the yard on the other side, and, incredible though it may seem, he had done it three times, I took his arm and led him home, lest in the end he should break his neck.

I had never seen such energy in a man. It was

unhuman. He was always impatient when walking, and was for ever wanting to run. He could not understand why we forbade him to gallop up the road with Delius in his carriage ! Despite his tremendous energy, he was rarely hungry, ate very little, was a non-smoker, non-drinker, and a vegetarian. Whilst we delighted in the pleasure of the table, he would sit with his bran and his glass of 'Château de Pump' — tepid water with a few drops of milk in it — and Delius would say, 'Jelka, stuff Percy well with oatmeal and macaroni; we know better, don't we, Eric ?'

On the first evening on which he played to us, I had walked through the corridor from Delius's bedroom to the music-room to tell Grainger that Delius was ready, when I was astonished to find him patting his knees furiously. Then, when he was black in the face, he sat back, calmed himself and was ready to play. After a very spirited performance of Chopin's B Minor Sonata — Delius's favourite work of Chopin — I ventured to ask him about that other performance, to which he replied that it was an exercise which he invariably did before going on to the platform. It consisted of four pats to the second, and this he kept up for a minute and a half. He must always feel excited before he could play.

I tried it for thirty seconds, and could not play at all !

The first time we played together he stopped me after a few bars and said, 'Fenby, you're a composer, are you not ?' I answered that I was fond of writing music, if that was the same thing.

'I thought so,' he commented. 'It's a theory of mine

that people like you all play alike; you do the same sort of things in your playing at precisely the same sort of places. I have noticed it again and again.'

Grainger was full of theories. There was scarcely a subject on which he talked (and he talked very brilliantly at times) without bringing in some pet theory of his – in fact, Delius said that he was 'bunged up with theories.' I could never understand his love of the harmonium as an instrument in the orchestra, and was amazed when he said, with all seriousness, that he wished the wood-wind of the orchestra could employ the perpetual *tremolo* of the cinema organ. During his stay with Delius he orchestrated his 'Hill-Song' for the fourth time. The pages of his scores were so thick with alterations, which had been glued one on top of the other, that Mrs. Delius used to say that one could have built houses out of them.

Grainger was extraordinarily frank about his own music, and claimed that Delius had been much influenced by it. Yet I never heard him boast. One afternoon on the river he told me, with the utmost nonchalance, that Beecham had said, 'Grainger, your "Colonial Song" is the worst piece of music I have ever set eyes on !' It was impossible not to admire the independent spirit of this charming Australian, even though one differed so greatly from him on most of the things he said, and, as I look back on those happy days, my chief recollection of him is his kindness. What could one say more of any man ?

In August of 1929 Evlyn and Grace Howard-Jones took a cottage in the village, and, having given the old peasant woman next door a few francs to wring the

neck of the lame cock-bird that woke them up before
sunrise, settled down peaceably for two months.

No sharper contrast could possibly be imagined
than that which existed between the playing of these
two celebrated pianists. Grainger played his own
works and those of Grieg with the wild gaiety of a
schoolboy, whereas Howard-Jones played with all
the classical control and restraint of a fine teacher.
Delius, although he loved it the least of all his works,
always contended that Howard-Jones's interpretation
of his Pianoforte Concerto was the best he had ever
heard.

The heat was now terrific, and one could not walk
with pleasure after seven in the morning until seven
at night. Almost every day there were loud beatings
of drums and blowings of trumpets to warn the
villagers of the approaching forest fires. For three
days it seemed that now we had touched the other
fierce extreme of an Inferno. Delius was in agony,
and work impossible. On the morning of the third day
the old gardener said that we should have a violent
thunderstorm that night, and, when the rain had fallen
in torrents and the air was fit to breathe again, it did
one good to look out over that summer garden all
ablaze with colour, and share its quiet, refreshing
mood – the mood that had so often inspired its owner
with thoughts of leisured musical loveliness.

Both Howard-Jones and his wife were ever ready
to come and play to Delius whenever he felt like music,
but it was not easy for them, for the works for violin
and piano that he could still listen to with enjoyment
were pitiably few in number.

Once when there had been some heated remarks about Beethoven's pianoforte sonatas, Howard-Jones had declared the Op. 110 in A♭ to be 'great music.' Delius challenged him: 'Well, play it, then !' And so it was arranged that on the following day, after tea, Howard-Jones was to play this sonata. Delius and I were seated beneath the open music-room window for this recital. All through the sonata the old man was restless, and frowned as he followed the music. 'Listen – listen,' he kept on saying and pointing excitedly with his finger the while (he could only do this when aroused). 'Listen – banal – banal – listen – listen, my boy – fillings – fillings !' When the music had ceased, and Howard-Jones had come beaming down the stairs to receive his bouquet, all he got for his pains was, 'Evlyn, why do you waste your time practising such rubbish ?'

Delius liked Howard-Jones, except when the latter began to discuss religion.

'Why ever does he want to argue about religion on such a lovely night as this ?' he complained in that slow and rather mocking tone into which he relapsed when one of those quips of dry humour (that passed his lips with never a smile) was on its way. He had just said good night to Howard-Jones following a lively argument during the evening walk, and, as I wheeled him in his carriage down the street, with the peasants all sitting at their doors and saluting us as we passed, I noticed with amusement that his hat was still at a rakish angle after he had accidentally knocked it so in a feeble attempt to brush a mosquito from his face.

'He reminds me of Runciman,'[1] he went on cantankerously. 'Runciman used to come purposely every Sunday when he stayed in Grez to argue about religion with me . . . and . . . well . . . you know, he knew I wasn't keen on Jesus !'

One morning in early August, as I was practising with Howard-Jones at his cottage for a concert we were giving that afternoon when Delius was to come to tea, Hildegarde, with cheeks redder than the apples in the orchard, burst in to say that Delius was in the garden and calling for me. Would I return immediately, as he was most impatient.

I found the old man sitting in his carriage by the stone table under the elder-tree down the garden, and looking like one possessed. He had thought out an entirely new opening for the work which is now known as *A Song of Summer*, and, having told me to fetch score-paper and pencil, and to imagine that we were sitting in the heather on the cliffs by the sea, he began to dictate. The following afternoon we went through the new opening at the piano, first at the proper speed and then slowly, and, when he had satisfied himself that every detail of the scoring was exactly as he would have it, I played through the whole work twice. The next morning, as soon as he had been carried down into the garden, he called for me to play it again, and, when I had gone downstairs from the music-room and joined him, he said, 'It's a good piece, lad ! Write the score out in ink.' He had barely uttered these words when the roundabout organ began. It was the fête day of Grez. The entire village was seething

1 John F. Runciman.

with excitement. The women rushed about preparing
an enormous mid-day meal, laying the great tables in
the shade of the courtyards of their houses whilst
their menfolk idled by the gates, gossiping and shaking
hands with relatives and friends from neighbouring
villages. When the feast was over, a peace descended
on the village, and even the roundabout organ took its
siesta. Then the children became restless, and began
to pour into the fair-ground. Gradually, from those
sweet beginnings, there rose up such a din as only a
noisy people like the French can make – ear-splitting
blasts on cornets and bugles, the high-pitched, jerky
songs with their silly tunes which the peasants bawl
at the top of their voices, the crack of a dozen rifles
at the firing-ranges, the raucous, penetrating voices of
the women, the coarse laughter and shouts of the
men, the screams of girls, and, above it all, the roundabout organ with its full-throated siren, and all this
commotion within a hundred yards of Delius's house !
Even the simple copying out of the score was impossible in this uproar, and, remembering that I was
little more than a boy myself, I went out into the
street, and round by the church up into the fair-
ground, and mingled with the crowd.

Our next visitor was that charming and genial
Irishman, Norman O'Neill. Delius had already
spoken of him with the greatest affection, and when
they were together I could see that O'Neill was one
of the very few people whom he loved. That impersonal, almost indifferent attitude which charac-
terised most of his human relationships left him
completely whenever mention was made of O'Neill,

and when I think of the way in which he looked
forward to O'Neill's yearly visits, and the delight with
which he relished his friend's amusing accounts of the
latest happenings in London – for the old man always
smacked his lips over a bit of good, honest gossip – it
is not strange that I can rarely think of O'Neill
without hearing in my mind that unaccustomed
friendliness which would creep into Delius's voice as
he said, 'Norman is coming,' or, 'I've heard from
Norman this morning.' It was as if he had suddenly
returned to the level of the normal balance of mankind. All the nervous tension and sense of detach-
ment that surrounded him, and made him so difficult
and inaccessible, save on rare occasions, seemed to
vanish with these words.

When O'Neill died with such tragic suddenness, the
old man was heart-broken. O'Neill was devoted to
Delius, though not blindly. Of all men, he knew his
Delius the man just as well as he knew his Delius the
composer. He told me that Fred's music meant more
to him than the work of any composer, past or present.

I, for one, will always remember him with gratitude,
for without his moral support and advice the difficulties with which I had to contend at Grez as time
went on would have been too much for me. He
understood everything.

Delius now announced his intention of ceasing
work. If he were to undertake the journey to England
to attend the festival – and up to the very last moment
he protested that, no matter by what easy stages he
was to travel, the strain of it would kill him – if he
were to undertake the journey in his state of health,

he must rest completely until the very day on which he was to start. Although Sir Thomas Beecham had written to say that he had made all the necessary arrangements for a motor ambulance to be despatched to Grez to take him comfortably by road to Boulogne, and from Folkestone to London, Delius still hesitated. Together with his wife, I played my part in persuading him to go. 'Delius,' said I, 'you have not heard the sound of the orchestra for all these years. Think of the thrill you will get when you hear your music in the concert-room again ! Isn't that enough temptation to risk it ?'

'Yes, yes, lad, I know,' he replied, 'but I haven't the strength, and when I die I want to die in Grez.'

Not until Sir Thomas finally took the bull by the horns, and came along in person from Fontainebleau to Grez, did Delius begin to entertain the idea with any seriousness.

It was just such another sweltering day as we had endured on the arrival of Percy Grainger when Sir Thomas, immaculately dressed, hat in hand, carrying an armful of scores and smoking an enormous cigar, stepped briskly into the courtyard, but, unlike his colonial friend, he took the very first opportunity of divesting himself of as much apparel as the laws of decency would admit, and permitted his taxi to wait nine hours for him at the door with all the disregard for triviality of the true *grand seigneur*. He soon settled the matter with dignity and calm, so that Delius had not a word to say. His mission achieved, he sparkled with his wine, and was gay and light-hearted as only he can be, poking fun at everything and everybody in music, himself included – a thing I have rarely heard him do. He explained that he had been advised to drink but little, and, on Delius's insisting, ' Do have another glass, Thomas,' he stood up, tested his foot carefully, and, pondering for a moment, as he fingered his beard, decided that it might stand another drop !

Sir Thomas had not brought his scores for nothing; he was memorising them for the festival. I knew very little in those days about those blue-pencilled markings that covered every page, but it was not long before I was to realise that in effect they meant all the difference between a good performance and a bad one. There was scarcely an expression mark in that whole armful of scores that he had not altered or modified. I saw that his energy and industry were alike prodigious, and when, afterwards, we had gone up to the music-room, and he was playing *Songs of Sunset* from a vocal score, and calling out all the orchestration to me as I sat beside him with the full score on my knee, I marvelled at the accuracy with which he retained the orchestral detail in his head.

A few days after Sir Thomas's visit I decided to leave Grez and await Delius in London. At lunch, on the day I left for England, the old man drank my health, and said that he would like to give me something in memory of that year. He called to his wife to place that something in his hand, and, supporting his hand on hers, he said, 'Take this and wear it for me, my dear boy. You have given me a new lease of life.'

I took his gift, fighting to keep back the tears, for of a sudden the laughter of the meal, the excitement of the festival, the coming music, my return the following year – all these things were forgotten, and I felt how near I had been to this strange man during the past year. I opened the box. It contained his gold watch and chain.

I SAW very little of Delius during the festival.[1] For the most part I was too busy helping Heseltine and Gibson, Sir Thomas's musical secretary at that time, in all the extra work that the festival entailed. Sir Thomas would come out from rehearsal and announce his intention of editing some score. Often he would mark it in the train on his way to conduct in the provinces, and send it back' with the guard on the next train so that we could get to work without delay. It was only possible for one person – two if you were extra polite – to delete the old markings from the parts and copy the new ones into the wood-wind and brass. The copyists could not be called in to duplicate it until a complete set of string parts was ready. Once when Sir Thomas caught me in the act of yawning in the green-room at Queen's Hall, he cocked his eye at me and said, 'Master Fenby, have you joined the night-shift ?' Indeed I had. Gibson and I had been working for nights at his office in Regent Street to the deafening accompaniment of pneumatic drills, fearful, too, lest we should suddenly be demolished with the premises next door. And now he had taken it into his head to edit the enormous score of the *Mass of Life* !

---

[1] The Delius Festival consisted of four orchestral and choral concerts (Oct. 12th, 18th, 26th; Nov. 1st) (Queen's Hall), and two chamber concerts (Oct. 16th, 23rd) (Aeolian Hall).

Still, there were occasional morning drives with Delius in Richmond Park, when, as at Grez, I described everything of interest as we drove along. Best of all there was the pleasure of seeing him so enthralled in the sound of his music in the concert-hall.

'You were right, Eric,' he turned to me and said, after the first work at the opening concert. 'How wonderful the orchestra sounds to me after all these years ! I am so glad I came.'

Delius was greatly touched by the warmth of his reception and the spontaneous kindness of his many friends and admirers.

Heseltine had the happy thought to bring his friend Augustus John along with him to the Langham Hotel, where Delius was staying as Sir Thomas's guest. John made a very fine sketch of the composer with lightning rapidity before going over to the concert with us.

I left Delius, after the festival, full of praise for Sir Thomas Beecham's masterly interpretations of his music, the magnificent playing of the orchestras taking part, and the fine singing of Kennedy Scott's Phil-harmonic Choir in the *Mass of Life*, which had brought the festival to a spirited close. In some of his purely orchestral works it had seemed that Delius had been listening to them for the very first time, so perfectly had their inner meaning been grasped and realised in performance. That was the way he wanted his music to be played – Beecham's way – and he hoped that the festival would do one thing above all else, and that, to establish a tradition by

G

which his music should live. If there was to be a
future for his music – and, despite his habitual
egotism, there were moments when he was curiously
humble about his work – it could only live in the tradition which Beecham had been at such pains to create.
The strain of listening intently to all the music of the
festival had tired him. He longed for the quiet of
Grez, and was most anxious to get back without delay.
'I shall expect you in the early New Year, my boy,'
he had said when I had taken my leave of him. 'By
then I shall be rested and able to work again.'

It was not until the end of January (1930), however,
that Delius dictated a note to me saying that he was
ready for work. I went out to him at once, but found
him racked with pain so that one could do nothing but
read aloud to him by the hour for days, whilst his
wife endeavoured to calm him as best she could. The
weather was mild, and there was nothing of that icy
cold that had made the previous winter so unbearable,
but there were heavy rains, and the river became a
raging torrent that flooded the meadows opposite
Delius's house until the lane to Moncourt was
impassable. It was scarcely light, for the sky was
dark and sinister with hurrying clouds. Each day I
went down on to the bridge, and when I saw the
villagers standing about in little groups, the men quiet
and thoughtful, the women in shawls, warning their
children not to go too near the edge as they gazed over
the waters, my mind instantly and always went back
to the many times I had stood among the fisher-folk
in the tiny villages of my native Yorkshire as they had
looked out anxiously over the cruel sea.

By the end of March, Delius had been well enough
to dictate his Third Sonata for violin and piano.
This was a comparatively easy task, and the composer
dictated it with astonishing rapidity. The few odds
and ends of sketches – the opening bars, a subsidiary
theme, and the germ for the second subject of the first
movement, a few bars of the second movement, and
the themes for the last movement – dated from the
war years, when concentration in Grez on a large work
was impossible. Several times, when the Germans
were nearing Paris, Delius and his wife had fled from
Grez, taking with them their beloved picture,
Gauguin's 'Nevermore,' and joined the sad procession
of refugees who night and day thronged the high road
from Fontainebleau. Once they had spent the night
in a cattle-truck.

When they could no longer bear the uncertainty and
the ever-loudening noise of the approaching guns,
they had buried the silver in the garden, disguised
and barricaded the stone staircase down to the wine-
cellar with innumerable barrow-loads of wood, so that
it looked like the approach to a wood-shed, and,
having crossed to England, had taken the boat from
Newcastle to Norway, where they had remained until
the Armistice. In their absence the house was used
as an English officers' mess, and, up there in Norway,
old Delius, like old Noah in Mr. Chesterton's poem,
must have 'often said to his wife when he sat down to
dine' that he didn't care what the soldiers did if they
didn't get into the wine !

Some of my sunniest recollections of Grez are the
wine-tasting days, which Delius always treated with

the greatest ceremony. I can picture him now, rolling that sensitive tongue of his round the wine, disputing other opinions, and pronouncing his own dictatorially. Although he could not see, I cannot remember him once confusing samples of a particular kind of wine that were somewhat similar in taste. He was as proud of his cellar as of his music.

The Sonata finished, Delius sent for May Harrison, asking her to come to Grez that Easter to play it over for him.

In the meantime Balfour Gardiner visited Grez, and this time brought with him his young friend, Patrick Hadley, the composer. It was decided that we should bottle the white wine, so Balfour Gardiner, with boyish enthusiasm, sat on a log pouring out the wine from a keg into the bottles with meticulous care, whilst Hadley corked them with a machine, and I wired them. The seventy bottles were then transferred in triumph to the wine-cellar. The next job that Mrs. Delius found for us to tackle was a very unsightly overhanging branch of a tree by the river. Gardiner thought it wise to have the boat beneath it, to steady the branch when it fell into the water. So, saying that he would bring the boat round from the boathouse, which lies in a tiny inlet at the side of the garden, he despatched Hadley and me to fetch a ladder and saw. When we returned, we expected to find him at the scene of operations with the boat, but, instead, there he was gyrating helplessly in mid-stream, and battling with one oar against the strong current about fifty yards away down the river. The boat had not been in use that winter, and the oars were still hanging in the shed. Apparently there had been an odd oar lying in the boat, and Gardiner had thought that he could paddle round that short distance to the tree with it. When we had recovered from our surprise and laughter, I shouted to him that if he could only manage to back-water, and keep to our side of the bridge, we would be on the bridge as soon as we could, and drop him the other oar as he passed underneath. So up the village street we raced, with the other oar, to the great consternation of the villagers; but, to our horror, when we reached the bridge Gardiner had already passed under it and was heading for the dangerous weir down by the mill. Fortunately, just as the situation was getting very serious, the inn-keeper, happening to be in his garden, and seeing Gardiner's plight, put off in a boat, and event-ually towed him into safety. Hadley then said that he would join Gardiner in the boat, so I remained on the bridge and watched their repeated efforts to pass under the farthest arch where the current was the slightest. At last they succeeded in getting through, but they were so exhausted that I called out to them to put into the side, where I would go down and take the oars. They took me on board, and all went well until, just as we were coming into the full force of the current, I missed my stroke, and back we shot under the bridge to where they had started. In the end, the innkeeper, a great, strong fellow like a prize-fighter, bared his enormous chest and, rolling his sleeves up, muttered something disparagingly about *les étrangers*. He seized the oars, took the bridge at the first attempt, and rowed the three mariners home.

Delius, of course, chaffed us unmercifully about it.

Needless to say, the offending branch remained undisturbed. Several weeks later, as I was wheeling Delius in his carriage down the garden, we heard a crash, followed by much shouting and cursing, and, going down to the water's edge, I discovered that the branch had fallen, and smashed up a fishing-party that had been lazing underneath. As soon as these excitable and furious Frenchmen saw Delius from out the wreckage of branches, bent and broken rods and tangled lines, their fury increased. It was all his fault. He must buy them new rods. But Delius merely answered in dry, unconcerned tones that it served them right. Hadn't they seen the notice on the tree, 'Défense de stationner'? These were his private fishing-grounds, and they had better be off before he called the *garde-champêtre*. They now presented a very sorry sight as they tried in vain to extricate themselves and to control the boat, which had broken away from its moorings and was drifting, wreckage and all, down the river. Then one of them missed his straw hat, and was livid with rage when another fisherman, in a boat anchored in the reeds at the other side of the river, roared with laughter and pointed to it as it sailed merrily before the wind about two lengths away. This was too much for him. Words jostled in his throat.

'If only old Lloyd George would look after his trees . . .'

'What was that?' questioned Delius, warming up to the fray. 'Lloyd George? Did he call me Lloyd George?'

I thought it was now time for me to intervene, so I whisked the carriage round and pushed the old man, now clutching his breast in his anger, out of sight.

As was always the case with Balfour Gardiner, he had no sooner arrived in Grez than he began to talk about leaving. All too soon Mrs. Delius and I were saying *au revoir* to our friends on the station at Nemours, our nearest town. Here we bought a *nasse*, a kind of big wire cage used for catching fish, and, slinging it behind the old Ford like some great double-bass, we returned home all agog with excitement, for I was determined to trap all the fish that had come up from the flooded river to the pond in the garden. But they were too clever for me, and all I could catch were water-rats, and, once, two frogs, the mother holding the little one on its back above water. I took the cage carefully out of the water, opened the wire door, and lifted the big frog out on to the ground somewhat gingerly with my handkerchief, putting its little one beside it. They both allowed me to handle them without the slightest sign of fear, and hopped off together in the long grass. Delius, when I told him of this, shook his head, and said that we should not get a wink of sleep that night 'for the "Hallelujah Chorus" of the frogs.'

It had come about that, during the course of conversation with Gardiner and Hadley, mention had been made of the full score and orchestral parts of Delius's early opera, *Koanga*, which had been missing for a great number of years. Nobody, it appeared, could trace them, yet Delius felt sure that they must be somewhere in London. 'Perhaps at this moment some grocer is tearing a sheet out of the score and wrapping up his butter in it,' Delius had suggested. However, Hadley had said that he would see what he could do. Perhaps they were lying in some publisher's warehouse, where they had been dumped by mistake. A few days later Hadley was back in Grez with the orchestral parts ! He had been right. Still, there was no trace whatever of the full score; they had searched everywhere. There was only one thing to be done, and that was to reconstruct the score from the material, for Sir Thomas Beecham had announced that he wished to play an excerpt from the opera. Having planted the orchestral parts all round the music-room, and threatened the servants with fire and brimstone if they did anything other than dust round them, I set about the colossal task myself. At first I found it a fascinating job always speculating as to what the next bar was going to be, but, after working the clock round for several days, the brain became dull, and one addressed oneself to this work for what it really was – nothing but mere hack work. Fortunately, there was no need for me to continue in this arduous way for more than a fortnight, for Hadley now informed us that, by a stroke of luck, he had unearthed the score. A new score had to be made, so I completed my copy from the original MS.

Easter brought May Harrison, and now we were able to hear the new Sonata. Delius was obviously very pleased with his achievement, and so delighted was he with May Harrison's musicianly interpretation that he dedicated the work to her. 'It seems a younger, fresher work than either of the other two sonatas,' said he, 'and in some respects I like it better.'

That May the garden, which had looked like a tiny corner of England with its well-trimmed flower-beds, pansies, forget-me-nots, wallflowers, its lilac and apple-blossom, and the soft mellow green of its trees, was suddenly white with snow. A blizzard swept the country, and the peasants said that the whole wine-crop of France would be ruined.

In early June there came a somewhat unusual visitor, a Scotsman from London named Erskine, who had been sent out to Grez by a friend of Delius, in the hope that he might be able to restore the composer's sight by the healing power of hypnotism. At first Delius would not hear of the suggestion, but he was eventually persuaded to try it. Erskine stayed a fortnight in Grez, and, though he did not succeed in his purpose, the results whilst they lasted were truly marvellous. Each morning he visited Delius and remained with him alone for over an hour. What the treatment was I do not know, but what I do know is that on the second day, when Delius took his walking exercise, with his wife supporting him on one side and his male nurse on the other, I saw him walk three times his usual distance without fatigue, and on the following day, instead of being carried from his carriage in the porch to his chair in the living-room, as was the custom, I saw him walk in like manner into the house, and not only walk with little aid, but go up the two steps into the living-room! Towards the end of the first week he could wipe his brow with his handkerchief, control his fingers sufficiently to take

his handkerchief from his breast-pocket and wipe his
nose, and touch his face with his forefinger, with
unerring accuracy, at whatever point Erskine in-
dicated. The amazing thing was that he continued to
do most of these things whether Erskine was present
or not. On our evening walks I observed that he
adjusted his hat himself, and, whenever a mosquito
settled on his face, he flicked it off with his forefinger,
when hitherto it would have had to have been done
for him. Yet, astonishing as all these things were –
for very few can realise how completely helpless he
was – there was still no mention of his seeing again.

Erskine was very friendly. He had not expected
to find 'an extraordinary man like Delius living in
such a god-forsaken hole as Grez.' He had imagined
Grez to be a fashionable little spa !

Delius, he confided, was the most difficult case he
had ever had. On the first day it had been no easy
matter to hypnotise him.

'I shall make him see before I go, but it will not be
for more than a few minutes at a time, if that. Perhaps
if he were to take a six months' course of treatment I
could make him see again permanently,' said he.

Erskine was very interested in music, and questioned me a great deal as to how Delius was able to
work with me. It seemed to him that there was
probably as much telepathy as intuition in it, if not
more, and, technical considerations apart, he certainly
did not think that I could have worked with such
understanding as Delius had credited me with had I
not lived with the composer so intimately for months
without a break. I, too, had often noticed during

working hours that a phrase that Delius was about to dictate had already occurred to me before he could name it. At some time or another of our lives we have all of us listened to a piece of music that we have not heard before, and been able to guess pretty well what the composer was going to do next, but that is not precisely the same thing. There, suggestion plays too great a part, and the brain, whether we are conscious of its functioning or not, is alert, and concentrated on the possible turns this new music might take; whereas at moments such as those to which I refer I was often writing out some passage as fast as I could, when like a flash some phrase would come to mind, and I would be amazed to hear Delius begin to dictate it.

It is true that during the course of work on a new composition I thought myself into it almost as much as did Delius himself. 'My dear boy, you finish my sentences for me,' he used to say. It was no use remaining passive and merely taking down the notes (even if one could have done at the speed at which he dictated), particularly with a man like Delius, who never repeated himself unless he could help it.

It will be remembered that earlier in the previous year Delius had had momentary glimpses of his hands at varying intervals over a period of several months, but to my knowledge these occurrences had ceased before he went to England for the festival, and there had been no mention of them ever since. Bearing in mind what Erskine had achieved in those few days, I was not surprised when, towards the end of the first week, they told me that Delius had seen his hands once more, but, as on those other occasions, only for an instant on awakening from his afternoon nap. Each day he saw for just such a little time, but no more, and by the middle of the second week Erskine as much as said to me privately that it was hopeless.

At the end of that week he came up to the music-room and said that he was going to bring Delius up. 'Don't go,' said he. 'I want you to remain.'

He then explained that he would like Delius to sit once more at a keyboard and finger the keys. Perhaps . . . but we would see. I hinted that Delius had not been able to play the piano for years, but he said that did not matter. What he was driving at I could not imagine. It seemed absurd, and I thought it a great mistake, but it was not for me to say so. I was preparing to put an armchair when Erskine stopped me.

'We'll use one of these instead,' said he, selecting a chair without arms. 'He'll sit on it all right!'

They carried Delius upstairs and set him down on the chair, but he could not sit on it unsupported, and I was sure that he would fall off. Erskine, however, went to him and steadied him, holding him gently by the shoulders.

'By the time I count five,' said he quietly, 'you will be able to sit on this chair without my help, but when I take my arms away you will not be able to move forward or say your name! One, two, three, four, five . . .' And with this he passed the tips of his fingers slowly down from Delius's head to his shoulders, and stood back. The old man could neither speak nor move, but exerted himself to his utmost to do so.

'Now say your name,' commanded Erskine after about half a minute of such struggling, and the old man repeated his name several times, and moved backwards and forwards in his chair as he was bidden.

'Now play !' ordered Erskine, and Delius lifted his hands unaided on to the keys, and there began a medley of meaningless sounds. Even in this terrible ordeal his sense of humour did not desert him, for he turned his head to me and said, 'Eric, the New Music !'

At this, I went over to Erskine and whispered that I had had enough of it, and left the room.

What is this awful power that some possess and others not, and what is this state called hypnotic sleep when a man is asleep yet awake ?

Whatever it is, and whether it comes from heaven or hell, let it be recorded that the great improvement which I have mentioned in Delius's general condition was maintained throughout that summer. That he was much less nervous and irritable was evident to everyone. I, for one, shall always be grateful to Erskine, in that Delius was now able to work day after day without interruption on his last choral work, which was to be called *Songs of Farewell*. Continuous work such as this was unheard of during those latter years.

Songs of Farewell, apart from its intrinsic musical merit, is a monument of what can be done when, the body broken, there still remains in a man the will to create. It should be an inspiration to every young composer who finds the spirit willing but the flesh weak.

It is a setting for double chorus and orchestra of words chosen by the composer's wife from Walt Whitman's *Leaves of Grass*. Here, in the first three movements, the composer gives voice to the 'silent backward tracings,' the 'meditations of old times resumed – their loves, joys, persons, voyages,' that delight the heart of man in the twilight of his days. The great forces of Nature are saluted in turn, and in the fourth and fifth movements, with a joyous leave-taking, the old sailor, bidding farewell to 'land and life,' speeds from the shore upon the endless chartless voyage of Death to the sound of the hushed voices of his friends in the final *pianissimo* chord, 'Depart !' A more cheerful note is struck at the thought of Death in this work than in the *Requiem*, the most depressing choral work I know.

So the months passed by uneventfully, except for a short visit from Beatrice Harrison and her mother which resulted in two pieces being specially written for her coming American tour – the Caprice and Elegy for 'cello solo and chamber orchestra.

That summer, Delius was particularly interested in the cricket test matches between England and Australia. Every morning, when I came down to lunch, I read to him the scores and the full account of each day's play. The progress of each match was watched with as much keenness as that of two spectators on the ground, and Mrs. Delius used to say that she had never heard so much talk about cricket as when her 'two Yorkshire lads' got together. And the old 'un used to brag how, in his prime, he had never let a loose ball go by without punishing it unmercifully, and never dropped a catch in the slips, and the young 'un used to believe him and tell how he had once skittled a team of yokels with his googlies for seven runs.

When, at last, the choral work was finished and all the slaving done, Delius quickly relapsed into his former state of utter ·helplessness and nervous irritability. Nothing we did was right, and I marvelled at the way his wife went on from day to day with such a happy heart in face of such difficulties. Every little change of weather affected him deeply, and once, when there had been a violent thunderstorm and one of the great trees in the garden had been left with a horrid scar from the lightning, there were days and nights of ceaseless pain for him and depression for us.

How Delius and his wife managed to keep their hold on life during such frightful times as these will always be a mystery to me. What he suffered and what she endured no one will ever know !

There must be something that comes with age to enable a man and a woman to bear the mental and physical strain of prolonged suffering and misfortune, for sensitive youth cannot stand up against it for long. I remember how, after days like these, I have walked about in the night and fought with myself to keep my sense of balance. Alone upon that great high road that for centuries has been a main artery connecting Paris with the south, I have peopled it in my imagination with the untold legions of the past: Charlemagne and his armies marching north; the merchants of medieval days coming up and down with all the outward splendour of their merchandise; the countless hosts of hooded friars with their staffs; Napoleon hurrying to Fontainebleau; and Balzac . . . had Balzac ever walked along by that lane through Hulay,[1] over the hill to Grez, when he was staying at the château lower down the road towards Nemours ? I wondered. To give full rein to the imagination in the quiet and cool of the night braces the jagged nerves like the healthy flush of the cleaner instincts that tone the body up when a man is astride a horse. These reflections brought forgetfulness, and I would return home ready for what the next day might bring. But this could not go on for long. When in the late autumn I had said good-bye to them, and was sitting in the taxi whilst my bags were strapped behind, I took one more glance through the door, into the Delius world beyond, and saw the last rays of the sun playing on the deep russet gold of the beech-trees in the garden (as in the love-scene of *Fennimore and Gerda*), and I sank back and felt like a worn-out old man.

[1] Hulay, a tiny hamlet near Grez.

11

Delius was very anxious to have Sir Thomas Beecham's opinion of the new choral work, so it was arranged that I should take the manuscript full score and play it over to him.

Sir Thomas was charming.

'Beautiful !' was his comment when I had finished playing the first number, and after the second he smiled and said 'Lovely !' When we had come to the last few bars of the work, he got up excitedly from his chair beside me and said, 'Ah, my dear fellow, this is lovely music; simple and direct and very much in the style of *A Late Lark*, isn't it ? But how the devil did you manage to get it down on paper ?'

'Extracting music from the brain of a Delius is not one of the easiest jobs,' I replied.

'No, I should think not,' said he, fingering his beard. 'I think you ought to be a Cabinet Minister !'

That was the Beecham touch, so I left it at that.

Christmas was clouded, for all of us who loved and admired him, by the tragic death of Philip Heseltine. Delius was greatly shocked and profoundly moved by the sad circumstances attending it.

'. . . the terrible tragedy of poor Phil has really quite unstrung me, and Jelka as well. We can think of nothing else,' he wrote.

He who has heard the cry of the curlew on a lone

and desolate moor has heard the music of this richly gifted personality. It is the saddest music I know.

For some months I was now busy in London, correcting proofs and orchestral parts, and interviewing publishers respecting all the new scores, but we kept up a constant exchange of letters, and I was constantly worried and alarmed by the unsatisfactory reports of the behaviour of Delius's male nurses.

The existence of such people was almost unheard-of in France, even in Paris, and, unless they had been able to read German fluently, Frenchmen would have been of little use, for not the least important part of their duties was the reading aloud, and Delius hated French. English male nurses were out of the question it seemed; all that remained were German. When, after endless searchings and unimaginable difficulties with the passport authorities, a new man was found, it invariably turned out that Providence had sent us a clown of the highest order. There were a few exceptions, but very few.

I had had a good deal of experience of these fellows, who were always threatening to leave at a moment's notice, and had often been truly thankful that poor Delius, the most fastidious of men, could not see them.

There was one in particular, who used to do the goose-step four or five times round the kitchen to get the right atmosphere before he entered the room. There was another who used to put dramas on our pillows at night, so that we might give him our considered opinion of his efforts by morning; and there was another who fell and crashed about like a comedian in pantomime.

One night, when this worthy had come to carry Delius up to bed, the old man said jokingly, 'Eric, just go upstairs and see if my bedroom door is open. You see, last night he carried me upstairs feet in the air and head on the ground. Then he swung me round at the top of the stairs like a battering-ram and pushed the door open with my head !'

I was not astonished, therefore, to receive the following letter:

'Grez-sur-Loing,
'11.5.31.
'3.30 a.m.

'MY DEAR ERIC, – As I am never sure to have a moment in the daytime, I will write to you now, as I cannot sleep. We have had the most troubled times with the new man all along. He was so extraordinarily unbalanced and unaccountable in his behaviour. Still we thought we must try to get along with him, after all the delay and difficulty of getting him into France.

'And do you know what happened ? On Friday afternoon after lunch he disappeared, and we have not seen him again. He ate a good lunch in his room, and brought down his tray, and that is the last that was seen ! In his room he left everything about, letters, clothes, his unmade bed, and an indescribable disorder. It was a rainy day, too, and I had had an awful time at Fontainebleau. He disliked poor Fred, and on Fridays there was generally some unpleasantness, but this time nothing special, and I had not spoken to him at all. We searched everywhere, and

M. Grespier went to the Gendarmerie at Nemours. No one saw him leave the house. At the stations of Nemours, Bourron, and Fontainebleau he was not seen. We could not help thinking of the river, as he was so moody at times – boisterous at others – but he had taken his money and passports, changed his blouse and put on an overcoat.

'Well, there we were with poor Fred and nobody to help us. The maids were very nice and carried him upstairs on a wicker chair, and I managed to do the rest somehow and get him undressed and fed him.

'Luckily I had felt that a catastrophe was brooding over us, and had got Mrs. Brooks to look out for a possible *remplaçant*, and I had also written to another of the former applicants who seemed so good. Through the American Hospital in Paris I got the address of a Canadian. I wired him to come, and he came yesterday afternoon to help us for a few days, and I am trying to get the other German to come as soon as possible as tourist. Then I will try to get him in *d'urgence*.

'I know you will understand what dreadful heart-ache and difficulty all this means to me, and the future so entirely uncertain. Also Fred got such a shock over his departure that he was not at all well. The weather was atrocious until yesterday, when it turned heavenly, and the Canadian helped to get Fred into the garden, where we had tea.

'The room of the man is all stacked with pamphlets, books on thought-reading, palmistry, Indian Yogi-ism, medicines, and treatises to fortify brain-power and give one great influence and power over people. That is probably what he tried to exercise over Fred in vain.

'The poor man had hardly any intellect at all, and all these silly theories nearly turned his brain. And where can he be ? I also wrote and enquired at the German Embassy in Paris.

'I always think of you, and especially when I go to look at the little chestnut, quite a tree now. Please write and tell us about everything.

'With both our affectionate love,
                              'JELKA DELIUS.'

I was very uneasy, and contemplated leaving my work and taking the next train to Paris. I wired, but there came no reply. However, I decided to wait, and news came eventually by letter. It read:

'Grez-sur-Loing,
                              '15.5.31.

'MY DEAR GOOD ERIC, – It was so dear of you to wire and offer to come and help me, and I thank you with all my heart. But I have help now. All happened most dramatically the day after I wrote to you.

'On Wednesday, a young German student of medicine wrote to me, recommended by the German Embassy. This man said that he would like to come and do the work, so I phoned at once and he was to arrive on Wednesday evening.

'Meanwhile at about 4 p.m. our lost man arrived, looking in a fearful state, and he had got the school-master to accompany him here. He hung his head

very much, and said an inner voice had called him
into the wilderness, so that like Buddha he could pass
through terrible times so as to purify his soul. He
rambled on like this and everybody was afraid he
would attack them. (The schoolmaster was very
nervous and had a revolver in his pocket.) But I saw
it was all gas and I took him to his room, where he
said, "Sleep, ah, sleep!" and sank on his bed and
was fast asleep at once. As he seemed perfectly mad,
I fetched André to put a bolt on our bedroom door,
and then, after a little while, he had washed himself,
and dressed like a tennis dandy in white flannels and
came downstairs to have a big meal. In the middle of
that, the new man arrived, a delicate little chap, and
very pale-looking.

'I had to rush out again and try and find someone to
escort the other man safely to the German Embassy in
Paris, and at last I got hold of C——, the brigand,[1]
who agreed enthusiastically to do the job. Now we
had to get the man to consent to leave and pack, and
we had another fright last night, as he had gone for a
walk and did not return. When at last he returned for
supper I quickly locked him in his part of the house.
Finally, this morning, he went off with R—— and the
brigand. We really cannot say if he is mad or simu-
lating. However, we are tremendously relieved to be
rid of him, and to have peace and harmony descend
upon the house once more. The new man has
already been assistant in a hospital; he understands
everything and learns very quickly. It was a wonderful

[1] This fellow, whom we nicknamed 'the brigand' on account of his red
face and flowing moustache, was a great local celebrity, and stalked about
the village like a Spanish desperado.

coincidence that he landed at the German Embassy just at the moment of our desperate need.

'With much love from us both, dear good friend,
'Yours affectionately,
'JELKA DELIUS.'

Thus we were all able to breathe freely again – until the next upheaval came along.

On September 17th of that year, Sir Henry Wood gave the first performance of *A Song of Summer* at the B.B.C. season of Promenade Concerts. Delius had written to Sir Henry saying that he would like me to play over the new work to him, and, when I had gone, and found him in his little room at Queen's Hall, bestrewn with orchestral parts and working in his shirt-sleeves at one of those menial jobs that most conductors leave to some wretched underling, I realised something of what I had heard of his pro-verbial thoroughness and untiring energy. The fol-lowing morning at rehearsal I felt very nervous as I listened to the work for the first time, for it must be remembered that Delius had never seen the score Happily I was able to wire to him that it sounded very well. *A Song of Summer* was given a good perfor-mance under Sir Henry, who delighted me by saying that he thought it a beautiful little work. He liked it so much that he had just made arrangements to include it in a programme he was to conduct in Belfast at the end of that season.

Immediately after this performance I returned to Grez. There I found the composer little changed in health, his wife looking worn and tired. He told me that he had 'listened in' to the new work with pleasure.

'It's a good piece, lad,' said he. 'I would have much rather heard it over again than my old Piano Concerto. I am so tired of it, and, as you know, I don't think much of it.'

It was during this visit that the score of the *Fantastic Dance* was completed by dictation, and this the composer dedicated to me. Another charming little piece written about this time was a prelude, *Irmelin*. This enchanting lyric for small orchestra arose out of a few musical ideas that particularly appealed to the composer in his very early unpublished and unperformed opera, *Irmelin*, and, slight though it is, I shall ever be sorry that Delius did not live to hear the lovely sound of it on the orchestra. It was one of the two pieces that Sir Thomas Beecham found it necessary to interpolate during a change of the scenery at the recent revival of Delius's third opera, *Koanga*, at Covent Garden. It is always fascinating to watch the reaction of the men in the orchestra during their playing of a new work for the first time. Usually the impression received by the onlooker as he scans the rows of faces is one of utter boredom and indifference. I shall nòt forget the smiles of approval and the delightful comments that accompanied its Lydian measures when Sir Thomas first rehearsed it at Covent Garden.

On my way home to spend Christmas with my parents, I had the good fortune to meet Elgar in London at the Langham Hotel. Sir Edward questioned me very searchingly about Delius, and the life he led at Grez, and deplored the death of Philip Heseltine. 'I can assure you, I felt it just as much as Delius,' said he.

I noticed that during the course of conversation Elgar persistently eyed my pocket, from which protruded the miniature score of his A♭ Symphony. Eventually I pulled it out and said, 'Oh, yes, I have just been listening to Beecham rehearsing this.'

'But I thought you young men didn't like that sort of thing,' he grumbled in rather suspicious tones, not taking his eyes from mine; it all ended in his autographing the last page of the slow movement for me.

'Do you know my *Falstaff*?' he enquired with considerable warmth. I replied that I did, and that, if he would allow me to say so, I considered it to be the finest piece of programme music ever written. He paid no heed to my remark, and went on proudly, 'I think it is my best work. Wait until you hear the gramophone records of it that I've just made. They're splendid!' When I left him he said, 'Come and see me whenever you like,' and then he added with a chuckle, 'And tell Delius that I grow more like Falstaff every day!'

That evening Beecham gave an exquisite performance of *In a Summer Garden*. The opening bars were poised to a nicety, and the timing of the oboe counterpoint, at the bar after the entrance of the strings, perfect. Usually the semiquaver notes of this fussy oboe figure are hurried in performance, so that at the very outset the spell is broken, and often the whole delicate machinery of the work thrown out of gear.

When we came to the Elgar Symphony I was unmoved. The third movement, that had once seemed the greatest slow movement in the whole range of symphonic literature, and which I had never tired of hearing, now seemed dull and uninspired, and its emotional appeal sickened me. It seemed hypocritical to have said what I had done to Elgar that afternoon and to feel like this, but such was the state of my nerves that, outside the world of Delius's music, I now felt strangely uneasy and unsafe. No young man could have lived for long periods with a man like Delius, as I had done, without having his sense of musical values constantly disturbed. Sometimes one felt that the only music that mattered was the music of Delius, and at other times one felt that one never wanted to hear a note of it again. Little did I realise how ill I was, and how soon I was to be prostrated with a nervous breakdown.

When word of this reached Delius, his wife wrote, 'Dear Fred had his eyes swimming in tears when I read him about your illness; he loves you dearly.'

By the following spring I was well enough to attend the final rehearsals for the first performance of *Songs of Farewell* at the Courtauld–Sargent Concert at Queen's Hall on March 22nd (1932). Delius had set his heart on a *première* under Beecham, but it was not possible to arrange this, and when Mrs. Courtauld went to Grez, and pressed the composer for its inclusion in the programmes that she was then drawing up for the coming season's series of concerts, Delius submitted, somewhat unwillingly, to her request. It was a very anxious young man who accompanied Dr. Sargent to the Royal College of Music, where the first full rehearsal was to be held. When I heard the sound of the tuning, and saw the Philharmonic Choir massed up behind the London Symphony Orchestra, and the audience of students, every one of whom had a score, I felt just as I had done at that first rehearsal of *A Song of Summer*, but, as on that occasion, I was afterwards able to wire to Delius that the new work had turned out well.

There was, however, this that worried me – the high soprano C at the climax 'Away, O soul, hoist instantly the anchor !' This was not the instance of a very high note coming in the stride of a work which otherwise kept for its intimacies within the middle compass of the voices, but a work in which even the quieter and more contemplative numbers were equally highly pitched. I do not think that it ever occurred to Delius that in these long rhapsodic passages the singers might need to take breath from time to time, any more than in a similar passage marked *fortissimo*, in a work like *A Song of the High Hills*, the trombone players might be given but one beat's rest in which to get their wind. Delius's entire output abounds in examples of this careless disregard for the limits of the human agency in performance. Again and again I had noticed, when working with him, that there was always a tendency in him to force up the pitch, particularly whenever the music became more animated. Sometimes he would even o'erleap his climax before reaching it ! I have often wondered whether to attribute this failing to the deafness in one ear which embarrassed his latter years, or to his lack of the sense of perfect pitch.

With Malcolm Sargent at the helm, *Songs of Farewell* began its adventure o'er the seas, and soon the old sailor was to depart upon his 'endless cruise.' His work was not yet quite finished.

12

ACH 'home-coming,' as Delius used to call my
return to Grez, was an occasion of great excitement in the household and frequent anxiety
for me, for it always happened that, shortly before my
departure, there would come a letter with a list of
eatables that I was to take. I have crossed the Channel
with muffins and pikelets, cheeses, Yorkshire ham
and bacon, sausages, jam, caraway-seeds, select blends
of tea, not to mention the night when, during a rough
crossing between Newhaven and Dieppe, the boat
reeking with the smell of new paint, I had oysters to
feed on the way !

This time, on arriving in Grez, in August (1932), I
found that delightful fellow James Gunn installed in
the studio above the music-room, and working on his
portrait of the composer which was to occupy so prominent a position in the following year's Academy. He
had come at the suggestion of Norman O'Neill, who
had persuaded Delius to allow his friend to paint him.
Gunn was working under great difficulties, for Delius
would only sit for short periods, and, even so, was
never still. Sometimes Gunn had no sooner fixed his
easel, and struggled down three flights of stairs with
his large canvas, when Delius would ask to be carried
away ! Then there was the problem of the light,
which could not be regulated; artist and sitter were
almost on top of each other. Delius would in no way

allow the sittings to interfere with the normal routine of his day, so that for the most part the artist had to struggle on as best he could. I felt sorry for Gunn, who was depressed by the atmosphere of nervous tension about the place, and I did my best to help him by deputising for the composer in a white shirt, open at the neck, and a white shoe which had to protrude a little from beneath the checked rug which Delius usually wore loosely over his knees.

The new male nurse had not turned out to be such a paragon after all, and was already about to leave. His temporary *remplaçant*, a meagre-looking Pole from Paris, was very nervous about carrying Delius, and Delius was still more nervous about being carried, so the poor fellow asked if he might practise on me before venturing on Delius. What with being carried up and down the precipitous spiral staircase by the little Pole, panting for breath, and posing for hours until the folds of the shirt and the innumerable checks of that confounded rug were completed, I could have out-Deliused Delius in irascibility by the time it was all finished.

Now that his unfinished manuscripts were completed, Delius said there was one more thing that he would like to do. Would I play him the score of his unpublished one-act opera, *Margot-la-Rouge* ? Perhaps something might yet be made of it. He had been badly in need of money, and had written this work in 1902 for a competition (the Sonzogno prize), one of the principal conditions of which was that the libretto must be of the French or Italian dramatic type, which he loathed. There had been very little time, and a

French authoress had offered him a libretto which, *faute de mieux*, he had accepted. When one remembers that *Margot-la-Rouge* is a product of those six magnificent years of passionate and vigorous creative activity when the composer was at the very height of his powers – 1900–1, *A Village Romeo and Juliet*; 1902, *Appalachia*; 1903, *Sea-drift*; 1904–5, *A Mass of Life* – it is not to be wondered at that now, those creative powers spent, he should turn back rather wistfully to this unfortunate work. His first intention, on hearing the music again, was to discard the original story – a sordid affair about a young French soldier's terrible vengeance when he finds his boyhood sweetheart, Margot, flaunting herself as a *fille de joie* in an infamous Paris café – and to ask his young friend Robert Nichols to write a new story so that he might drastically revise the score. Later, however, he decided to retain only such sections of the work as particularly appealed to him, and to adapt them to a selection of words from Walt Whitman that Nichols had compiled for him. The prelude to *Margot-la-Rouge*, evoking, as it does, the presence of a distant metropolis, suggested the retrospective line, 'Once I passed through a populous city,' and the work gradually assumed its present form, an Idyll for soprano, baritone, and orchestra. A short orchestral introduction, the original prelude to the opera, leads to the baritone entry:

> 'Once I passed through a populous city,
> Imprinting my brain with all its shows.
> Of that city I remember only a woman,
> A woman I casually met,
> Who detained me for love of me.

> Day by day and night by night we were together –
> all else has been forgotten by me.
> Again we wander, we love, we separate,
> Again she holds me by the hand, I must not go.
> Day by day and night by night together !'

Then, in his musing, he hears the voice of the woman :

> 'Day by day, night by night we were together,'

he crying :

> 'I hear her whisper,'

and she, singing again :

> 'I love you, before long I die.
> I have waited long merely to look on you,
> For I could not die till I had once looked on you.'

They extol the contentedness and solemnity of their ascent to the 'sphere of lovers,' and the music becomes more and more impassioned :

> 'O to speed where there is space enough and
> air enough at last !
> We are two hawks, we soar above and look down.
> What is all else to us, who have voided all but
> freedom and all but our own joy ?'

But, as in *Songs of Sunset* :

> 'They are not long, the days of wine and roses,'

the dread of separation darkens as a cloud :

> 'Face so pale with wondrous eyes, gather closer yet,
> closer yet.
> Perfume therefore my chant, O love, immortal love.
> Make me a fountain
> That I exhale love wherever I go.'

The work ends with a beautiful yet poignant passage:

Man: 'Sweet are the blooming cheeks of the living.
　　　Sweet are the musical voices sounding,
　　　But sweet, ah, sweet are the dead
　　　With their silent eyes.'
Woman: 'I ascend, I float to the regions of your love, O man.'
Both: 'All is over and long gone, but
　　　Love is not over.'

When Delius dictated the last line of the baritone part, I smiled but made no comment. Several months later, when the score had been published, apropos of a remark he made I pointed out tactfully that that phrase might have dropped out of *Songs of Sunset*. Greatly taken aback, he had not noticed it until then.

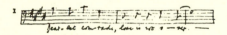

Thus does a composer repeat himself unconsciously under stress of similar emotions.

The Idyll was first performed at the Promenade Concerts on October 3rd, 1933, under Sir Henry Wood, Dora Labette and Roy Henderson being the soloists.

The dreary monotony of that winter[2] was broken at intervals – all too few for me – by visits from Cecil Gray, Arnold Bax (both rather silent and shy, but always stimulating when they did talk), Kenneth Spence, with whom Delius loved to recall his wanderings in Norway, and Professor Dent, whose book on Busoni was now in print, and which we had just read

---

[1] See p. 69.　　　[2] 1932–3.

aloud to Delius with the greatest interest. Gray in particular was almost as astonished by the extraordinary liveliness of Delius's mind as was Spence by the amazing accuracy of his memory, but the professor remarked that he could not forget how greatly Delius had aged since his last visit two years before.

The other visitor was Lionel Tertis, who came to play his viola arrangement of the Third Sonata for violin and piano to the composer. Tertis, like most people, had imagined Grez to be but a very short distance from Paris, whereas it lies about six miles beyond Fontainebleau, which town is already about thirty-eight miles from Paris by road. The taxi-driver – the rogue ! – was apparently also under the same impression. Village after village they passed, battling their way through a blinding snowstorm, poor Tertis shivering and anxious on the edge of his seat, clattering at the window to urge the scoundrel on. After two hours of such agony they at last pulled up outside Delius's house, and Tertis, clutching his viola, entered, a picture of desolation. He had no feeling in his hands; how could he possibly play, he said; besides, that fellow had swindled him abominably. After a while, however, we managed to thaw him, and he went up to the music-room and played as only a great artist can play. Rarely had I seen Delius so happy. One of my most treasured possessions is the beautiful letter which Tertis wrote after his visit, complimenting me on my playing with him without a rehearsal.

It was during a short and unavoidable absence from Grez, attending to matters respecting the publication

and first performance of the Idyll, that Elgar paid
the composer a visit. It had interested me to hear
from Sir Edward, whilst I was yet in England, that
he was 'happy at finding Delius so bright.'

Delius described their meeting to me as follows:

'Elgar came. It was really delightful. He stayed
from tea-time until nearly seven o'clock. He was very
genial and natural and altogether quite unlike what I
had expected him to be. I never knew him well.
I had seen him for a moment now and then in London
and once at the Birmingham Festival in 1912 when he
conducted a new thing of his – *The Music-Makers*, I
believe. Anyhow I didn't care for it – it was too
rowdy and commonplace. That was the time they
did *Sea-drift* and Sibelius came over to conduct a new
work of his, the Fourth Symphony – fine music with
a genuine feeling for Nature. I like Sibelius, he's a
splendid fellow. I had often met him at Busoni's
house. Elgar brought me an album of his records –
the Fifth Symphony, *Tapiola*, and *Pohjola's Daughter*
– very good in their way, but he always uses the same
procedure to get the music going and that irritates me.
A lot of his work is too complicated and thought out.
I've got no use for that sort of writing. I've written
pages of it myself – paper-music – but I had the sense
to burn them. If you knew the amount of music I've
written and burned you would be amazed. It is
against my nature to write music like that. The
English like that sort of thing just as they like vogues
for this and that. Now it's Sibelius, and when they're
tired of him they'll boost up Mahler and Bruckner.
There's an album of Wolf songs that Elgar also

brought. I've played one or two on the gramophone, but I never liked Wolf. Herbert Janssen sings them beautifully with the deepest feeling, every syllable declaimed perfectly, with just that graveness of voice that gets to the very heart of the words, but what a sad and morbid fellow poor Wolf must have been ! I've never been able to understand why people like Ernest Newman rave so much about his music !

'We talked about music. I told Elgar that I had just finished the Idyll with your help, and he was very interested in the way we managed to work and asked a great deal about you. He said he was sorry that he'd missed you. He then went on to say that he was busy working on his Third Symphony.

' "But then," he added, "my music will not interest you, Delius; you are too much of a poet for a workman like me !"

'I replied that I thought there was some fine stuff in his Introduction and Allegro for strings, and that I admired his *Falstaff*, but I thought it was a great pity that he had wasted so much time and energy in writing those long-winded oratorios.

' "That," said Elgar, "is the penalty of my English environment."

' "Well, anyhow, Elgar, you're not as bad as Parry," I replied. "He would have set the whole Bible to music had he lived long enough !"

'We talked about books (and I could see that he was very well read), about people we'd known, about what would grow in my garden and what would not grow in his in England. He was as excited as a schoolboy about his first trip from Croydon to Paris by air and

insisted that, should I go to England again, I must
travel by air. He would love to conduct some of my
music. Would I send him some scores ? I said that I
would and that it would give me the greatest pleasure.
We had a bottle of champagne before he left, and I was
very disappointed that he couldn't stay longer, but he
had to motor back to Paris to see young Yehudi
Menuhin that night.

  ' "The way that boy plays my concerto is amazing,"
said Elgar. Obviously I could see that he adored the
youngster. Most of the time he sat close by me on a
very modest chair, the one my man generally uses,
and, as Jelka afterwards told me, he constantly tele-
graphed signs to her – was he tiring me ? – was he to
leave ? – but, of course, she negatived them. Yes, I
liked Elgar very much. . . .'

              .   .   .   .

  I now found myself in a very difficult position at
Grez, for, although the music was finished and my
mission ended, Delius insisted on my staying on with
him. In the house of a healthy man I should have
been happy to do so, for then I could have worked,
but it was irksome for a young man to go on regulating
his life according to the whims of a sick man. Those
five years had taught me that it is not wholesome and
good for a youngster to live for long periods in an
atmosphere of sickness and depression if he would
keep his spirit, and the doctors had told me that,
cared for as he was by his wife, there was no reason
why Delius should not live for yet another ten years.
With the best intentions, the attitude of both Delius

and his wife had become so possessive towards me that they strongly resented my friendship with anyone outside the household. Accustomed even as I was from childhood to solitude, I could no longer bear the sad loneliness of Grez devoid of all young society. My position was further complicated by Mrs. Delius, who was now showing evident signs of fatigue. She had not been well for some time, owing to an accident in which she was knocked down in the dark by a drunken cyclist, and, but for my presence of mind, would have been killed by a passing motor-car. However, on Delius's saying that he would ask his niece, Peggy, to come and stay with them to relieve Mrs. Delius with the reading, I decided to leave Grez, but on the understanding that they were to send for me should anything serious occur.

It was with the greatest satisfaction that I afterwards heard that my parents had received the following letter:

'Grez-sur-Loing.
'12.7.1933.

'DEAR MR. AND MRS. FENBY, – These are only a few words to thank you once more for letting us have Eric so long ! The work he has done for me is absolutely unique, and it is almost a miracle that he came at all and that he worked so admirably.

'I want you to know how deeply we feel and appreciate what he has done. He has always been so steadfast and painstaking, and with his wonderful musical gift added to all those good qualities he has achieved it. It seems so glorious that all these works that but for him would have remained mere sketches are now actually brought to life and in the publishers' hands.

'I hope that now Eric will start his own work and achieve great things ! We miss him very much indeed.

'With kind remembrances from my wife to you both,

'I remain,

'Yours affectionately,

'FREDERICK DELIUS.'

PART TWO

HOW HE WORKED

IN attempting to show how Delius worked by dictation, it must not be supposed that I am dissecting the printed scores as I know them to-day. The only way in which I can give some idea of the method of work is for me to forget the pages of the scores which I have chosen for my illustrations, so to speak, and put them together again as Delius dictated them to me. I must therefore imagine myself to be in turns both creator and amanuensis: the creator who knows what he wishes to be written down, the amanuensis who has little or no idea of what is to follow. It is obviously impossible for me to remember the exact words that Delius used at each dictation, but, as I live it all over again, my memory serves me well enough to vouch for the accuracy of the order and the way in which the detail was assembled at the actual time of composition, and the picturesque remarks which that detail often brought forth.

The technique of dictation varied, often considerably, with each work. Much depended on the extent to which Delius had already arranged and sifted in his mind the musical matter of what he was going to say before calling for me to note it down. Sometimes he had no more than the roughest idea of what he wanted until that rough idea had been played over to him at the piano. The final test was always the sound of his musical thought when transferred to the piano. With the exception of the solitary occasion which I am about to describe, Delius always worked in the music-room, I sitting at the keyboard and playing each dictation for his correction or emendation before writing a note of it into the score. Again and again the work of several days proved to be but a mere stepping-stone to something finer. Delius was never able to think of and retain more than a few bars at a time, and the most he ever dictated at a stretch was the new opening to the orchestral work *A Song of Summer*. It will be recalled that the good material from the rejected MS. *A Poem of Life and Love* was turned to account in *A Song of Summer*; that Delius was still dissatisfied with the opening; and how I found him sitting in his carriage under the elder-tree waiting for me to take down an entirely new opening, which, he said, had come to him in the night.

It happened like this:

'Eric, is that you ?' he called, as he heard me coming down the garden path. 'I want you to write down this new opening for the new work. Bring your score-paper and sit beside me. . . .

'I want you to imagine that we are sitting on the cliffs in the heather looking out over the sea. The sustained chords in the high strings suggest the clear sky, and the stillness and calmness of the scene, $\frac{7}{4}$ in a bar (four and a three); divided strings, chord of D major – A, D, F♯ doubled at the octave, lowest note the A string of the violas. Dovetail the violin parts (F♯ and D), (A and F♯), and mark the score "Lento Molto" and each voice *pianissimo*. Hold the chord for two bars.'

Example 1 shows what I wrote down, and each

subsequent example
gives the progress of
the score as I con-
tinued to write from
bar to bar.

'You remember
that figure that comes
in the violins when
the music becomes
more animated' –
sings it. 'I'm intro-
ducing it here to
suggest the gentle

rise and fall of the waves. Now the fifth beat of the

first bar 'cellos and basses in octaves in quarter notes'
– sings and calls out names of notes – 'G♯, A, D, C
(hold it – a whole note), then repeat the same.'   As I
was scribbling this down, he went on, 'Slur the
quarter notes – one bow, and with each rise and fall
put crescendo and decrescendo marks.'   Ex. 2.

'Now go on with the 'cellos, again in quarter notes
– bottom F♯, tar-tar-tar – hold it' – sings – 'last note
seven beats.'   Ex. 3.

'What have we got in the basses ?'
'F♯, B, C♯, F♯, seven beats,' I sing.
'Good; where was I with the upper strings ?'

'At the beginning of the third bar.'

'The same chord again, a new bow, and move down to E in the firsts on the last quarter note, then up to A (five beats)' – sings – 'Tar – tar, tar, tar. Keep the F♯ in the second fiddles running right through.' Ex. 4.

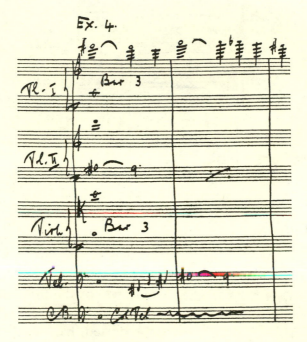

Ex. 4.

'Now, on the fifth beat, change the chord. A's to B's and D's to fifths (F♯, C♯) and come back to the same position of the D major chord at the next bar and hold it through the bar. Strengthen the viola F♯ at the change of the chord at the octave in the second fiddles. Swell out all voices up the bar and soften down the next.' Ex. 5.

'A whole note chord at the new bar; C, A, violas; octave F♯s, second violins; A, F♯ firsts; move each voice down a tone except the first halves of the first fiddles and hold for a dotted half note and tell me what you've got.'

'B♭, G, violas; octave E's, seconds; and G in the second halves of the firsts.'

'Good.' Ex. 6.

'Now add octave C in the first halves; mark it "Divisi." Next chord – violas, F♯, E♭;

seconds, octave C's; E♭, second halves of firsts; and move the divisi octave down to B♭. Hold it seven beats.' Ex. 7.

'Now, after that chromatic passage in the firsts' – sings it – 'Tar – tar, tar, tar – I want a semi-quaver run up in tones in the solo flute from top D to A, three beats on A, and then come down – ti, er – ti, er' – sings the phrase – 'hold it for the rest of the bar. The ti, er figure is the same value as the one that comes in that solo oboe passage later on' (sings it). Ex. 8.

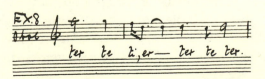

K

'Is that ti, er in the flute G♮, Delius ?'
'Yes.'   Ex. 9.

'That flute figure suggests a seagull gliding by.   Now put a horn call on the fourth beat of the last bar' – sings it – 'and the same progression in the strings moving from a whole note chord at the beginning of the next bar, violas G, E; octave C♯s in the seconds; E♮ second halves of the firsts; octave A, divisi first halves.'   Ex. 10.

Ex. 10.

'What have you got for your last chord?'
'D♭, B♭, violas; octave G's in the seconds; B♭,
second halves of the firsts; octave F, first halves.'
'No, that won't do! Make a note of the chord for
the next bar, C♭, F, 'cellos divisi; A in the violas; E♭,
seconds; A, firsts.' Ex. 11.

'Alter the distribution of that other chord; Db, second 'cellos; G and Bb, violas; F and G, seconds; Bb and F, firsts.' Ex. 12.

'Bring the F's down to E on the last beat of the bar. Now the next bar, the chord I've already given you, move the Cb in the 'cellos down to Bb for a dotted half note on the fifth beat, and the other voices a beat after; no, I'm wrong, the Eb in the seconds

Ex. 12.

should move down to D on the fifth beat (a quarter note) and then to a half note C#.'

I sensed that he wanted a 7-6 progression over the 'cello Bb and that the chord on the first beat of the following bar

would be relative to the chord of F, so I tried to help
him out:

'First violins, A to a half note G; violas, A to B♭;
'cellos, F to E.'

'That's it; now a strong chord held through the bar,
A and D in the 'cellos, fifths in the violas (F and C)
non-divisi; C and F in the seconds and the same
phrase as we had at the beginning in the firsts, Tar –
tar, tar, tar – hold it seven beats' (sings it). Ex. 13.

'Now go back and give that flute counterpoint to the
oboe, beginning the bar after the horn call; you'll see
at a glance how it fits. The first note is A (second
space), and repeat the horn call (first note to sound
B♭).' Ex. 14.

'Have you got that?'
'Yes.'

'Go on to that long note in the first violins, the same chord but C in the 'cellos; F in the violas (first line); A and D, seconds; and let the basses double the 'cellos at the octave from that C onwards. That same waving figure again' – sings it – 'and change the upper strings to Bb, F, A; F, fourth space in the violas;

Bb below the stave, seconds. Mark that bar *piano*
and repeat it *pianissimo* and 'cellos and basses hold the
D through the bar.' Ex. 15.

'Now, two more bars to lead into the $\frac{3}{2}$ movement.
Violas, D and F♯; second violins, B♮; 'cellos, D
below the stave and A, first space; basses, in fourths,
you know what I mean ! First horn, three half notes,
then a quarter note' – sings the phrase – 'and repeat
in the next bar. At that bar bassoons at same pitch
as violas playing same notes solo.' Ex. 16.

'Bring the bassoons down a semitone in thirds on
the last beat, and give the 'cellos and basses the same
rhythm as the bar before that strong chord' – sings it –
'ter – ter, ter – ter. Take the octave A's in the 'cellos
and basses down to G♯ at the beginning of the last
bar and go down chromatically to end on F♯ on the
first beat of the $\frac{3}{2}$ movement in that rhythm.' Ex. 17.

EX. 16

'It would be an improvement if, in the first bar, you changed the F♯ in the violas on the fifth beat to F♮. Give those two notes, F♯ to F♮, to the second horn, and that seagull figure to the flute again. This time vary it. Start the flutter up from D (fourth line), the first ti, er – (G♯), and the second one upwards this time' (sings it).

'You mean D, F♯ ?'

'Yes. Repeat the flutter up on the bassoon in the last bar, starting from B (the same note as the solo horn), and at the ti, er – come down from E♯ to C♯.' Ex. 18.

At the end will be found the complete passage

Ex. 17.

after it had been played over to the composer at the piano, improved here and there in detail and finally set up in print.

The foregoing remarks must not lead the reader to think that composition by dictation proceeded in

a calm and leisurely way. On the contrary, the
composer dictated with great rapidity, and with one
or two exceptions – for instance, the closing bars of
Songs of Farewell – the accompanying mood was one
of frenzy and great physical activity. He could not
keep still, but would wriggle about in his armchair,
gesticulating wildly with his hands to a degree that
would have been impossible in a more collected mood
until, bathed in perspiration, he could go on no longer.
Then he would be carried away exhausted. This new
opening to *A Song of Summer* was the easiest of all.
We will now turn to a more difficult undertaking –
the second movement of *Songs of Farewell*. Of this,
the orchestral introduction (Example 20) already
existed in short score. Note the 'backward tracing,'[1]
the theme in the horns in the last two bars, which
plays a prominent part in the development of this
short movement.

[1] *Hassan.*

Delius, having memorised the words, set to work as follows:

'First, I want you to read the words to me, then play the opening.'

I began:

'I stand as on some mighty eagle's beak,
    Eastward the sea absorbing, viewing (nothing but sea
        and sky)
    The tossing waves, the foam, the ships in the distance,
    The wild unrest, the snowy, curling caps – that inbound
        urge and urge of waves,
    Seeking the shores for ever.'

I now played over the opening. At the last bar he called out, 'Now then, go on – "I stand as on some mighty eagle's beak" – chord of C.' Here I played the particular disposition of the chord that I had in mind, but he corrected me – 'No, the top note E, not C! – now hold it – "Eastward the sea" – change the chord at "sea," B♭ in the bass, and reach out to top G, hold it – "sea absorbing, viewing nothing"; at "nothing," change the chord – A major, "nothing but sea and sky." '

After playing this, I jotted it down.

He then went on:

'Now, to suggest the rolling of the sea, go backwards and forwards on each half note – C♯, C♮, C♯, C♮' (sings and calls out the notes). ' "The tossing waves" – octaves in the basses A, B minor in the right hand; keep the C♯; now work up – ter, ter, ter, ter' – sings B, A, C, B excitedly – 'that's it, F in the bass – "the foam" – now then, up !' – sings the note and I feel my way with chords.

When I was not writing during his dictation I was feeling my way at the keyboard, striking every note immediately after he had named it, and anticipating whenever possible what I thought would be the next chord as well as my musical instincts and his verbal directions would allow me.

But to continue:

'Yes, yes, that's it !' he went on, 'now move the left hand up chromatically and mark it "trombones." "The ships in the distance" – move the whole chord up – yes – now what comes next ?'

' "The wild unrest !" '

'Strong chord on the brass; what's your last bass note ?'

'B.'

'Move up to chord of C – "the wild unrest" – on "unrest" change the chord, that rolling movement again, E to E♭; A in the bass. Mark that a *sforzando* chord in the horns. "The snowy, curling caps" – a swaying movement ⁶₄ in a bar – now C, E♭, G, B, keep the inner parts and move up to C in the treble and down to A in the bass and repeat. Now same thing a half note lower and change the harmony.'

At this point I fumbled about badly, not knowing precisely what he meant. After a time I stumbled on the right progression, and quickly wrote it down, for he was already ahead – ' "that inbound urge and urge of waves" – down to F♯ in the bass, chord of B – no, up to F♯, that's it; hold the F♯ – A in the bass, minor chord – "and urge" – now on the second "urge" hold the chord and go down to E in the bass – "urge of waves" – on "waves" come down to E, A to G♯ – yes – but play C♮, not C♯ – "seeking the shores for ever" back to C major on "seeking," and on "shores" go up to G.' Here he sang the soprano phrase 'shores for ever' and left it at that.

'Now play the whole thing through from the beginning and recite the words when you come to them.' Example 21 will give some idea of what I played.

When I reached the 'shores for ever' he called out,
'Now come up from C below the line in the 'cellos
rather like the opening' – sings the phrase – 'and come
down chromatically in sixths with the seconds. Move
the bass in quarter notes and the sopranos in half
notes on shores.' Ex. 22.

'Now repeat that last phrase in quarter notes in the
strings and keep the inner parts moving chromatically
– no, no, down a whole tone in the bass and lead into
the opening theme in the 'cellos.' Here he sang each
part ahead whilst I endeavoured to reproduce the
progression at the piano. Ex. 23.

That was enough for one day.

At the next two sessions he shaped the chorus parts
from the crude chunks of sound of Example 21,
gave more definition to the movement of the chords,
and sketched the ending. Ex. 24.

I wondered what he would do with the horn theme
(bars 10 and 11 of the introduction) and was not
surprised when he said that he wanted it to 'run
through the movement,' first in the wind, then in the
strings. The tiny interjections by the flute were meant

Ex. 24.

to 'suggest the tints of white on the crests of the waves' (bars 2, 3, and 4 of the $\frac{6}{4}$ movement). Example 25 should make that clear.

Ex 25.

At 'sky' he inserted another bar of that 'rolling' movement (from C♯ to C♮), and said that after that bar the strings should take up the horn theme, but before doing so they must ascend gradually in octaves to the high C♯ after 'sky,' beginning at the word 'viewing.' Having dictated this, he freed the basses at 'the tossing waves' and added a trumpet note *sforzando* at 'foam,' to 'give a touch of fire to the colouring.' The 'horn theme' was then developed in the high strings as shown in Example 26.

These rough sketches in short score were now dispensed with, and we began to work in full score. The pages at the end of the book give the patient reader the whole movement as he hears it in the concert-room.

These illustrations, the opening of *A Song of Summer* and the second movement of *Songs of Farewell*, remain most clearly in my mind as two of the few instances in which Delius appeared to know fairly accurately the notation of the music he wished me to write down before a note of it had been realised in sound at the keyboard. An account of what happened when he felt moved suddenly to compose without premeditation, as it were, would be unreadable, even if what I have already attempted is readable, were I to describe it here.

Such was the way Delius worked during his last years of fitful creative activity.

Such, too, was my privilege in helping him.

Ex. 26 follows

Ex 26

PART THREE

SOME ASPECTS OF
THE MAN AND THE COMPOSER
AS I KNEW HIM

WHAT can we know of any man ? And, when all is said and done, how little do we understand those of whom we boast that we can read them like an open book. We tack on to some obvious idiosyncrasy, some loose remark, some stray gesture, and from these things we draw our host of vain conclusions, good or evil, according to the measure of our nature. Seldom do we realise in our everyday dealings with others that the simplest nature is an unfathomable mine of complexity, responding in incalculable ways to the subtle probings of that infinitude of things that makes this life of ours what it is, and even though we may sometimes remember this, we are all too prone and eager to forget it.

There are some who say that knowledge of the man behind the work of art is unnecessary, and they are probably right, for few of us improve on closer acquaintanceship. Yet there are others who, the more they hear or see of a work of art, the more keenly are they interested in the man, the mind of the man who created it, and the conditions and circumstances under which it was created. This, I think, is a natural and healthy curiosity so long as a true sense of values is maintained. That is not easy in this godless age; it is well-nigh impossible. A constant, almost superhuman effort is required if one would detach oneself yet mingle freely with the throng and preserve intact one's innocency of vision.

Man of himself can create nothing. The impetus for creation is not of this world, this world that 'is too much with us,' and it is just because there are so few who have spiritual insight into things not of this world that our sense of values is so easily warped. Again, how few there are who can appreciate a work of art without conjuring up in their minds a picture of the super-man who fashioned it by giving that impetus from within the form they now enjoy. Let them give the creator the homage and gratitude he deserves for developing the powers that distinguish him from his fellows, and for the diligence with which he has turned that mysterious inner driving-power to beautiful account. But let them not make a god of him, for these creators are apt to turn out, after all, to be mere men, with the failings of men, like the rest of us. It is a sad reflection on the prevailing spirit of our times that it should be necessary to deplore such a false attitude of mind. That it exists, in a much more general degree than is usually supposed, has long been painfully evident to me by the absurd comments that I have heard from the mouths of so many people concerning Delius. The moment they began to talk about the man, it seemed that they had lost all sense of proportion.

The musician Delius was greater than the man Delius. He lives for us now in his music, and not by reason of his outstanding qualities as a man. I doubt whether we should ever have heard of him apart from it.

What was extraordinary in the man as I knew him was not so much that which was inherent in his nature (as with a man like Beecham, who would have excelled in almost anything to which he had applied that remarkable brain of his), but that which was largely the fruit of his Unbelief and the secluded life he found it necessary to lead in order to perfect his art, namely his intellectual isolation, his inhuman aloofness, his penetrating truthfulness, wholly indifferent thereby whether he hurt people or not, his utter contempt for 'the crowd,' and his all-embracing self-sufficiency. To these were added his colossal egotism, his dreadful selfishness, his splendid generosity (particularly to those of his old friends who had fallen on hard times), his equal indifference to money and honours, his exceptional refinement, and his noble triumph over an almost total physical incapacitation.

That he was a true artist if ever there was one, none can deny. Everything and everybody were subservient to the chief business of his life – his music. That was the only thing that mattered. The rest could go.

It was fortunate for him and for us that he met and married Jelka Rosen when he did, otherwise we might also never have heard of him as a musician, for he was not one of those men who can organise their lives. She did it for him, and it was no easy task.

Their first meeting had not been very promising. She had known that he was a composer, and he had said that he loved Grieg's songs; she had offered to sing some for him. He had winced when she had started and been polite when she had ended. The discovery that they had a common interest that dominated their lives – their mutual enthusiasm for the philosophy of Nietzsche – gradually drew them together in a way that nothing else could have done.

It must not be imagined that Delius had always been the country dreamer that the music of his maturity would seem to suggest. There had been a wild and reckless youth spent in the great cities of the world, with much travelling over half the earth, and many love-affairs, and one, the affair of his life, which had come to nothing. There had been no inclination to settle down in the country now that his studies at Leipzig were completed. On the contrary, he loved the Paris of those days, and the gay and picturesque Scandinavian students there who were so vital to his happiness. The men liked him; the women adored him. But there were moments when he felt he must get away from the market-place; that that noble urge to creation which he felt within him, which alone seemed worth while, and which set him apart from other men, must be preserved at all costs.

The three months that he had spent entirely alone on his orange-grove in Florida before going to Leipzig had been a revelation to him. 'I was demoralised when I left Bradford for Florida,' he told me; 'you can have no idea of the state of my mind in those days. In Florida, through sitting and gazing at Nature, I gradually learnt the way in which I should eventually find myself, but it was not until years after I had settled at Grez that I really found myself. Nobody could help me. Contemplation, like composition, cannot be taught.'

Since those days when the stillness of nature had first calmed the troubled waters of his soul, he had known in his heart that he had something to give, something to say about life in terms of music that no one else could give or say.   This noble urge which stirred him so strangely was the only spiritual thing in life for which he had reverence, and this remained so unto the end of his days.

The second call, as he himself confessed, was a call to a much more complicated being than the mere boy who had sailed for Florida.   That first call had been a call of the boy to the man in him; the second call should have been the call of the man to the boy in him. But it was the call of the man to the man in him, the call of Nietzsche's super-man, Zarathustra.

Open still remaineth the earth for great souls.   Empty are still many sites for lone ones and twain ones, around which floateth the odour of tranquil seas.

Open still remaineth a free life for great souls.   Verily, he who possesseth little is so much the less possessed: blessed be moderate poverty !

There, when the state ceaseth – there only commenceth the man who is not superfluous: there commenceth the song of the necessary ones, the single and irreplaceable melody. . . .

Flee, my friend, into thy solitude !   I see thee deafened with the noise of the great men, and stung all over with the stings of the little ones.

Admirably do forest and rock know how to be silent with thee.   Resemble again the tree which thou lovest, the broad-branched one – silently and attentively it o'erhangeth the sea.

Where solitude endeth, there beginneth the market-place; and where the market-place beginneth, there beginneth also the noise of the great actors, and the buzzing of the poison-flies. . . .

Little do the people understand what is great – that is to

say, the creating agency. But they have a taste for all repre-
senters and actors of great things. . . .

Full of clattering buffoons is the market-place – and the
people glory in their great men ! These are for them the
masters of the hour. . . .

Slow is the experience of all deep fountains: long have they
to wait until they know *what* hath fallen into their depths. . . .

Flee into thy solitude ! Thou hast lived too closely to the
small and the pitiable. Flee from their invisible vengeance !
Towards thee they have nothing but vengeance. . . .

They flatter thee, as one flattereth a God or Devil; they
whimper before thee, as before a God or Devil. What doth it
come to ? Flatterers are they, and whimperers, and nothing
more.

Often, also, do they show themselves to thee as amiable
ones. But that hath ever been the prudence of the cowardly.
Yea ! the cowardly are wise ! . . .

Because thou art gentle and of upright character, thou
sayest: 'Blameless are they for their small existence.' But
these circumscribed souls think: 'Blamable is all great
existence.' . . .

In thy presence they feel themselves small, and their
baseness gleameth and gloweth against thee in invisible
vengeance.

Sawest thou not how often they became dumb when thou
approachedst them, and how their energy left them like the
smoke of an extinguishing fire ?

Yea, my friend, the bad conscience art thou of thy neighbours; for they are unworthy of thee. Therefore they hate
thee, and would fain suck thy blood.

Thy neighbours will always be poisonous flies; what is
great in thee – that itself must make them more poisonous,
and more fly-like.

Flee, my friend, into thy solitude – and thither, where a
rough strong breeze bloweth. It is not thy lot to be a fly-
flap. . . .

Ye higher men, learn *this* from me: On the market-place no one believeth in higher men. But if ye will speak there, very well! The populace, however, blinketh: 'We are all equal.'

'Ye higher men' – so blinketh the populace – 'there are no higher men, we are all equal; man is man, before God – we are all equal!'

Before God! – Now, however, this God hath died. Before the populace, however, we will not be equal. Ye higher men, away from the market-place!

Before God! Now, however, this God hath died! Ye higher men, this God was your greatest danger.

Only since he lay in the grave have ye again arisen. Now only cometh the great noontide, now only doth the higher man become – master!

Have ye understood this word, O my brethren? ye are frightened; do your hearts turn giddy? Doth the abyss yawn for you? Doth the hell-hound here yelp at you?

Well! Take heart! ye higher men! Now only travaileth the mountain of the human future. God hath died: now do *we* desire – the Superman to live.

No matter what the motive, withdrawal from the world, if even for but a brief period, has usually been the first step that a man has taken on the road to high endeavour.

At such times of tremendous inner conflict Delius would pack his bag and lose himself in the country for weeks together, thinking only of his work; and, when he could bear that no longer, back he would come to Paris and plunge again into the whirlpool of life. Not that he was lazy. Even amid the thousand and one distractions of Paris the habit of regular work which he had acquired from Ward, out there in Florida, never left him. That virtue was the surest defence against a nature and temperament such as his, and it saved him. Ward, a devout Catholic and his senior by a few months, had known his pupil for what he was – a headstrong, boisterous, hot-blooded young fellow with more than a streak of the adventurer in him – and he had taken him well in hand.

I remember my amusement when, on turning over the pages of an illustrated edition of the complete works of Byron bearing the inscription 'From Thomas F. Ward, Jacksonville, Florida, to Fritz Delius, Leipzig, Germany,' I found the following passage heavily scored and marked by a pressed flower:

> The youth who trains, or runs a race,
> Must bear privations with unruffled face,
> Be call'd to labour when he thinks to dine,
> And, harder still, leave wenching, and his wine.

Speaking of those early days, Delius once said to me, 'It was not until I began to attend the harmony and counterpoint classes at the Leipzig Conservatorium that I realised the sterling worth of Ward as a teacher. He was excellent for what I wanted to know, and a most charming fellow into the bargain. Had it not been that there were great opportunities for hearing music and talking music, and that I met Grieg, my studies at Leipzig were a complete waste of time. As far as my composing was concerned, Ward's counterpoint lessons were the only lessons from which I ever derived any benefit. Towards the end of my course with him – and he made me work like a nigger – he showed wonderful insight in helping me to find out just how much in the way of traditional technique would be useful to me.' After a pause, in which he appeared to be deep in thought, he added, 'And there wasn't much. A sense of flow is the main thing, and it doesn't matter how you do it so long as you master it.'

Unhappily, Ward did not live to see his pupil famous, but died of tuberculosis, after spending the last years of his short life in a monastery.

A quiet, regulated country existence, then, was not very much to the taste of this fiery young Delius, still in his early thirties, but he felt that if he was to find himself, and realise his ambition as a composer, no other life was possible. It meant sacrificing a great many things without which, mistakenly enough, he thought he could not live, and it was not done all in a day. Long after he had settled at Grez-sur-Loing, Delius was ever clamouring to be off to Paris. After a few days of concentrated work on some score, he would suddenly come downstairs from his music-room, surprise his wife at her painting in the garden, and announce his intention of taking the next train to Paris. He wanted a change.

A woman possessing less tact and understanding would have made many a scene, but she knew that he would eventually see for himself the futility of all this gadding about for half the night on the Montparnasse with companions, most of whom were worthless.

Delius was a very fortunate man in most respects. It was always his good luck to meet precisely the very people he needed at the crucial stages of his career. First there came Ward, who gave him a sound grounding in his art; then Grieg, who encouraged

M

him with his friendship and practical advice, and to whom he continued to send his scores for comment after he had left Leipzig; then Jelka Rosen, to whom he was well mated, and who made it materially possible for him to devote himself entirely to composition; and, lastly, Beecham, who did everything that a man could do to establish his genius.

As I see it, it is a tragedy that Ward's influence was a purely musical one. Would that, together with those seeds of musical culture, Ward could have sown but a few of the Catholic culture, not so much as to make his pupil a Catholic, but, at least, a believer; for with belief there would have come that joy which is not to be found in his music, and which constitutes its chief defect. What joy there is, is as an echo through the ages of the joys of pagan antiquity – the joy of the gods, and the delight in all natural things before the world was born again. It is tinged with the sadness with which all joy must be tinged that is not born of that virtue which Christianity brought into the world – hope. And there is no hope in Delius's music.

'Lift up your hearts, my brethren, high, higher !' sings Zarathustra in the *Mass of Life*, 'and do not forget your legs ! Lift up also your legs, ye good dancers, and better still if ye stand upon your heads ! This crown of the laugher, this rose-garland crown: I myself have put on this crown, I myself have consecrated my laughter.' For all this, he cannot exult, nor can he dance, and the faintest flicker of a smile never crosses his face.

Despite its undeniable grandeur, its strength, its

moving passages of ravishing beauty when the poetry
of both poet and composer is at its most musical, I
have never yet come away from a performance of the
Mass of Life without feeling depressed.   I am not
alone in this.   Several others have had like experience.
Better, as one of them said, somewhat irreverently,
had it been called the *Mess of Life*.

Already as a youth, when he had left Bradford on
his first visit to Florida, Delius was at heart a pagan.
A young mind, such as his, that had been nurtured
chiefly on detective stories and penny dreadfuls, was
not likely to forget that incident he had witnessed in
Bradford when Bradlaugh had stood, with his watch
in his hand, calling on his Creator·to strike him dead
within two minutes if He existed !   Delius had never
forgotten that two minutes.   It had made a lasting
impression on him.

When, one wet day, a few years later, he was
looking for something to read in the library of a
Norwegian friend with whom he was staying during a
walking tour, and had taken down a book, *Thus Spake
Zarathustra* – a book, for all and none – by one
Friedrich Nietzsche, he was ripe for it.   That book,
he told me, never left his hands until he had devoured
it from cover to cover.   It was the very book he had
been seeking all along, and finding that book he
declared to be one of the most important events of his
life.   Nor did he rest content until he had read every
work of Nietzsche that he could lay his hands on; and
the poison entered into his soul.

Given those great natural musical gifts and that
nature of his, so full of feeling, and which at its finest

inclined ιo that exalted end of man which is contemplation, there is no knowing to what sublime heights he would have risen had he chosen to look upwards to God instead of downwards to man ! It was just the difference between upwards and downwards, but what a difference ! 'Ye look aloft when ye long for exaltation, and I look downward because I am exalted,' says Nietzsche's Zarathustra. It is this looking downward that chains Delius's music to the earth.

There are many for whom this music is too much of the earth earthy. None would have complained had it been too much of heaven heavenly, for no music can be too heavenly. It is the lack of heaven in the minds of its creators that is the curse of music. As yet we have no standard of comparison by which the truth of this may be judged. Oh, for a modern Palestrina to breathe into the voices of the modern orchestra the music of that joy of joys, that blessed felicity that would transport us with an earthly tasting of eternal bliss !

If, following the way of the great Christian contemplatives, Delius had chosen to look aloft, he would have brought heaven to earth, for, constructing music as he did by feeling alone within the structure of his particular sense of form, and with his delicate touch and refinement, he would have been the perfect composer for those long flights of musical felicity which none have attempted, yet which I pray I may hear from some composer ere I die. Such music, when it comes, will be the music of Eternal Life.

It is a confession of the utmost spiritual poverty of

soul to maintain, as so many moderns maintain, that the possibilities of music have been exhausted. Of the higher realms of spiritual exploration music has said very little; of the highest realm, next to nothing at all. This is strange, yet not strange. Strange, because music is of all the arts the one and only art that can give expression to the mystery of heavenly things, the one language in which the inexpressible is expressible, and not strange in that the creation of the kind of music that I am trying to define, and in which Delius would have excelled, would demand rare qualities of mind and disposition in the soul of the creator.

> Music some think no music is
> Unless she sing of clip and kiss,
> And bring to wanton tunes fie fie,
> Or ti-ha ta-ha or I'll cry,
> But let such rhymes no more disgrace
> Music sprung of heavenly race.

That is rather an excess of zeal, for a balanced life of action and contemplation is as essential in the ideal type of composer as in the anchorite, but the poet had the root of the matter in him. Let composers write as much active music as they may, and hard necessity will see to it that they are not failing in this, but would that more often they would practise that higher contemplation, not, as with Delius, finding their chief inspiration in the works of God, but, in the words of one of the greatest of all mystics – John of Ruysbroeck – in 'the most noble and the most profitable contemplation to which one can attain in this life,' the contemplation of God Himself.

'Man,' says Ruysbroeck, 'created in the image and after the likeness of God, has a natural tendency towards God, because of the spark of the soul, and because of the highest reason, which always desires the good and hates the evil.

.   .   .   .

'And he shall raise his enlightened eyes, by means of the illuminated reason, to the intelligible Truth, and mark and behold in a creaturely way the most high Nature of God and the fathomless attributes which are in God: For to a fathomless Nature belong fathomless virtues and activities.

'The most high Nature of the Godhead may thus be perceived and beheld: how it is Simplicity and One-foldness, inaccessible Height and bottomless Depth, incomprehensible Breadth and eternal Length, a dark Silence, a wild Desert, the Rest of all saints in the Unity, and a common Fruition of Himself and all saints in Eternity. And many other marvels may be seen in the abysmal Sea of the Godhead; and though, because of the grossness of the senses to which they must be shown from without, we must use sensible images, yet, in truth, these things are perceived and beheld from within, as an abysmal and unconditioned Good. But if they must be shown from without, it must be done by means of diverse similitudes and images, according to the enlightenment of the reason of him who shapes and shows them. The enlightened man shall also mark and behold the attributes of the Father in the Godhead: how He is omnipotent Power and Might, Creator, Mover, Preserver, Beginning and

End, the Origin and Being of all creatures. This the rill of grace shows to the enlightened reason in its radiance. It also shows the attributes of the Eternal Word: abysmal Wisdom and Truth, Pattern of all creatures and all life, Eternal and unchanging Rule, none of which is hidden from Him: Transillumination and Enlightenment of all saints in heaven and on earth, according to the merits of each. And even as this rill of radiance shows the distinctions between many things, so it also shows to the enlightened reason the attributes of the Holy Ghost: incomprehensible Love and Generosity, Compassion and Mercy, infinite Faithfulness and Benevolence, inconceivable Greatness, outpouring Richness, a limitless Goodness, drenching through all heavenly spirits with delight, a Flame of Fire which burns all things together in the Unity, a flowing Fountain, rich in all savours, according to the desire of each; the Preparation of all saints for their eternal bliss and their entrance therein, an Embrace and Penetration of the Father, Son, and all saints in fruitive Unity. All this is observed and beheld without differentiation or division in the simple Nature of the Godhead.'

The way of this 'most noble and profitable contemplation,' this 'perpetual striving after the unattainable,' this 'swimming against the stream – busy in ourselves, idle in God,' this 'seeing and beholding of Truth which,' says St. Augustine, 'is the seventh and last stage of the soul (and not indeed a stage but a habitation to which she attains by these stages),' Ruysbroeck describes with exceptional clarity and directness: 'But if above all things we would taste God, and feel eternal life in ourselves, we must go forth into God with our feeling, above reason; and there we must abide, onefold, empty of ourselves, and free from images, lifted up by love into the simple bareness of our intelligence. For when we go out in love beyond and above all things, and die to all observation in ignorance and in darkness, then we are wrought and transformed through the Eternal Word, Who is the Image of the Father. In this idleness of our spirit, we receive the Incomprehensible Light which enwraps us and penetrates us, as the air is penetrated by the light of the sun. And this Light is nothing else than a fathomless staring and seeing. What we are, that we behold; and what we behold, that we are: for our thought, our life, and our being are uplifted in simplicity, and made one with the Truth which is God. And therefore in this simple staring we are one life and one spirit with God.'

If Delius had understood contemplation in this traditional and Dionysian sense, what a musician we should have had ! He would have been unquestionably the greatest composer of his generation, and the most inspiring composer who ever put pen to paper. With what serenity he sang of the loveliness that is fast passing away before our eyes, of creaturely happiness short-lived, never more to return. But we need to forget the misery of this our exile, and be made mindful of the happiness which is our destiny. With what serenity would he have sung had he beheld 'God in all things, without distinction, in a simple seeing, in the Divine brightness' ! He had no faith in God, no faith in his fellow men, only a proud and simple faith in himself. All through his self-guided life he was blind to what he was doing, blind in the highest sense of the word, directing his untiring energy to the worship of Pure Beauty as a supreme end in itself, instead of to that end of ends which is God.

Such an opinion, for what it is worth in these days, would have once seemed sound and normal to the generality of men, who saw things unconsciously through the light of a common faith. Now all that is gone, and it is unlikely that it will find favour anywhere, least of all in the Delius camp. I am well aware of the ridicule that it will bring on my head. Nevertheless, I shall hold to it tenaciously, knowing that, should I live to be an old man, I shall still think the same, and my admiration for Delius's music will in no wise have suffered thereby.

From my very first days in Grez I tried desperately hard to understand Delius and his attitude towards life, and all through the years there I was ever careful to avoid the slightest mention of religion. Religion, like health, is never harped upon save by the unhealthy.

My position was not easy, however, for as time went on the old man gradually grew to take a fatherly interest in my mental development. 'You must always tell me what you think about things,' said he one evening (several months after I had been in Grez), as I wheeled him up the hill out of the village in search of coolness. 'Perhaps I may be able to help you.'

I should have been very communicative about many things other than music had he not killed all my desire to be so by a remark which he made a few days later. We had been talking about Haydn, and I had said that I thought he was a much greater composer than most musicians seemed to admit; that I was most anxious to hear a performance of his *Creation*. I had seen the score, and been so amazed by the many modern touches in the instrumentation that I had laughed with delight. 'There is one enchanting passage, Delius,' said I, 'that always makes me wish that I had known old Haydn every time I think of it. It goes, "And God created great whales, and every . . ." ' '

'God ?' interrupted Delius. 'God ? I don't know Him !'

This was not all.

Shortly afterwards, during another evening walk, apropos of something we were discussing, he said, 'Given a young composer of genius, the surest way to ruin him is to make a Christian of him. He will end up by being a second Perosi. Look at Elgar. He might have been a great composer if he had thrown all that religious paraphernalia overboard. *Gerontius* is a nauseating work, and, of course, tremendously influenced by *Parsifal*.'

I made no comment on either of these occasions.

Again, after he had been particularly pleased with the quickness with which I had taken down some music, he hinted that he was really very disappointed in me. It was a pity that I was 'one of the weaklings.'[1]

The climax, when it did come, burst over me like a thunderclap. Robert Nichols had been paying

[1] Referring no doubt to the 'weaklings' in his Pagan Requiem who, filled with woe and fear, drugged themselves with dreams and golden visions, and built themselves a house of lies to live in.

Delius a visit, and there had been a great deal of talk about Nietzsche between the two in the garden on the day on which Nichols had left. I had kept silent. That evening, when we were alone, without the slightest warning, Delius turned on me like a lion: 'Eric, I've been thinking. The sooner you get rid of all this Christian humbug the better. The whole traditional conception of life is false. Throw those great Christian blinkers away, and look around you and stand on your own feet and be a man. We are all sent into this world, we know not how and we know not why. We each have our own individualities, our own particular and varying natures, and our job is to find ourselves at all costs. Never be afraid of being yourself in spite of everything and everybody. Be yourself, and don't trouble if it hurts anybody else. They'll soon get over it. That is the supreme test of a man – his ability to stand on his own. Look to yourself, and don't narrow and hedge in your life with conventional behaviour and all these silly moral restrictions that are the stupid invention of priests. Sex plays a tremendous part in life. It is terrible to think that we have come into this world by some despicable physical act. Don't believe all the tommy-rot priests tell you; learn and prove everything by your own experience. Do things and find things out for yourself, and don't be frightened of making a fool of yourself. If an unmarried girl came to me and said she had had a child, I should say, "My girl, you have done well." Take Christianity. Jesus was a beautiful character – if He ever existed – but if He was the Son of God, whatever that may mean, there was no merit whatever in His perfections, for in that He was God He set up an impossible ideal for man to imitate. I am inclined to think, along with Brandes, that the whole thing is a myth, like William Tell. One thing is certain – that English music will never be any good till they get rid of Jesus. Humanity is incredible. It will believe anything, anything to escape reality. We shall probably find in the end that man is no more than a mere vegetable. The whole system of things as we know it is a vast speculation. Tell me, what Catholic ever wrote a piece of music worth hearing ?'

'But, Delius,' said I, 'what about that romantic thing that sprang from the very heart of the Catholic Church – plainsong ? When it is unaccompanied and sung with understanding, as it so rarely is, it never fails to move me. For me its power to move is almost as mysterious as the very nature of music itself.'

'I see no mystery in it,' replied Delius emphatically, 'just dullness; and you are evading my question.'

'Well, consider Palestrina and Victoria, two of my favourite composers and both devout Catholics,' I pleaded. 'You must admit that a motet like Palestrina's *Laudate Dominum* is an astounding piece of music.'

'What ! Do you call theirs fine music ? You should have said mathematics,' he snapped.

'I grant you, Delius, that these two composers have been the cause of more musical snobbery than all the rest of them put together. I have heard people go into raptures over modern performances of Palestrina, when they should have been either helpless under the seats with laughter or completely distracted. I admit that there are times when both Palestrina and Victoria can be as dull as old Bach.'

'And don't I know it,' put in Delius, with something of a sneer in his tone.

'I'm speaking of their inspired pages, not when they functioned as mere craftsmen without having anything vital to say,' I continued.

'No, my boy, it's no use,' concluded Delius, 'you'll never convince me that music will be any good until it gets rid of the Jesus element. It has paralysed music all along.'

I argued that I did not see how a disciplined intellect in the harness of a strong and simple faith could harm any artist. Besides, one could not dismiss the religious experiences and intuitions common to men of all ages as things unworthy of consideration, but Delius merely replied that all artists were 'best rid of such nonsense.'

The following Christmas he sent me a copy of *Thus Spake Zarathustra* with the accompanying note: 'In introducing you to Nietzsche my intention is to open up new horizons to you. I myself do not subscribe to everything Nietzsche said, but I hail in him a sublime poet and a beautiful nature. I want to make myself very plain to you as regards religions and creeds. Personally I have no use for any of them. There is only one real happiness in life, and that is the happiness of creating.'

I did not get along very well with Zarathustra. I was prejudiced before I started, for it was my misfortune to come across some of Nietzsche's music.

Whatever he may have been as a philosopher, whatever he may have been as a poet, the Reverend John Bacchus Dykes, that infallible touchstone in matters of this kind, and without mention of whom no essay on Delius would be complete, was a veritable Mozart compared with Nietzsche as a composer. Since then I have never been able to take the fellow seriously.

Delius knew nothing of this, for he had the profoundest admiration for the man and his work, so much so that I often thought it was Nietzsche himself addressing me. Sayings such as these that come haphazard into my mind as I write: 'Christianity preaches Death.' 'There is little difference as far as I can see between animals and the great mass of humanity. They live to feed themselves and take as much as they can from others. Man is the cruellest animal.' 'Sin as we know it is an invention of the Jews.' 'To pity is to be weak. Don't let your heart run away with you or your head will soon be chasing it.' 'The state you call chastity is responsible for as much filth of soul as lust.' Sayings such as these, which sounded so novel and striking to a young man's ears, and particularly when a Delius had finished rolling his tongue round them, had all found perfect expression, had I then known it, in the rhapsodic utterances of Nietzsche. Many a time I discovered that they were word for word the same. It was not until Delius told me that it had been his habit, over a period of a great many years, to open *Thus Spake Zarathustra* at random, take a chapter and ponder over it sometimes for weeks together, then, when he had extracted its essence, turn to another and do likewise, that I realised something of the influence Nietzsche had exercised over him, and something of his disappointment in my polite refusal to follow his example.

The occasion of this outburst was the only one on which there was ever anything approaching unpleasantness between us, yet to the end he continued to taunt me for my persistence in being a Christian. Every time I went down to lunch or supper I was always in danger of heavy bombardment. If, during the reading of the day, he found anything that he could shoot against me, he would ask his man to give him the signal on my entrance to the room, and open fire before I had passed through the door.

Once, when the guns were loaded, and the enemy had come into the room unobserved and surprised the sentry drowsing over his reading and the gunner snoring louder than the reading, the sentry, astonished, and faithful to his orders, gave the signal in a loud voice:

'Herr Delius, Herr Fenby ist dar !'

No response.

The battle-cry was now transposed into a higher key:

'Herr Delius, Herr Fenby ist dar !'

'Vas ist es ?' yawned Delius, coming to with a start.

'Herr Fenby ist dar !'

There was a pause, and I waited for the barrage to begin. It opened like a sudden clang of the heavy orchestral brass.

'In 1755 there was an earthquake in Lisbon. Thirty thousand people were destroyed in a few minutes !

How do you reconcile that with your loving God who is supposed to mark the fall of every sparrow ?'

'I know, Delius, it is very hard; very hard indeed to understand the meaning of these things,' I replied quietly.

'Then why do you believe as you do ?' he questioned severely.

It was now time to unload myself of a shot that always exasperated and silenced him, a remark made by Dr. Johnson; when 'talking of those who denied the truth of Christianity,' he said, 'it is always easy to be on the negative side.'

'Damn Dr. Johnson !' he would say, and, clutching his breast, wriggle from side to side in his anger, and invariably would mutter something about the man's intelligence being 'sadly overrated.' I dreaded these encounters, for they always unsettled him until he had slept them off.

Seldom did he miss an opportunity of poking good-natured fun at me in the presence of others. Once, when in the company of several distinguished musicians, he had ordered the wireless to be switched on, and none of them, himself included, knew the name of the work, nor the composer of the work that was being played (one of those appalling effusions the equivalent of that shocking taste in devotional objects which make most of our churches a purgatory on earth for sensitive people), he suddenly said, 'Go and fetch Fenby. He'll tell us what it is. He knows all about angels !'

There was, however, towards the end of my time at Grez, one other occasion on which he was furious with me. Apparently he thought I was paying too much attention to a very charming young English girl who was known by the lovely name of Soldanella, and who happened to be staying for a short while with her father, a great friend of mine, in the village. Having returned one afternoon from a stroll in the forest with her, I was told that Delius wished to speak to me privately on a matter of great importance. I would find him at the bottom of the garden. As I came round the corner by the bamboos, I saw him sitting there in silence beneath the great trees with his head back, facing the sun, his man raiding an apple-tree near by. I walked across the lawn and greeted him with the usual, 'Here we are, Delius.'

'Eric,' he began sternly, with his usual outspokenness on such subjects, whether he was in the presence of his wife or not, 'what are your intentions towards Miss —— ? Marriage ?'

'But, Delius,' I explained, 'I hardly know the girl !'

'Well, you must never marry,' he continued severely. 'No artist should ever marry. He should be as free as the winds. Amuse yourself with as many women as you like, but for the sake of your art never marry one. It's fatal. And listen; if you ever do have to marry, marry a girl who is more in love with your art than with you. It's from your art only that you will get lasting happiness in life, not from love. Love is a madness. The physical attraction soon plays itself out. Passionate affairs are like fireworks flaring up only to fizzle out. You are a fool if you ever marry.'

I thanked him for his advice, and took up my book and began to read.

N

Mention has been made of his absolute truthfulness, and how he always said exactly what he felt regardless of the feelings of others. He often upbraided me because I thought a more moderate course was sometimes the better part of discretion. A very tiresome habit of his, and often a very embarrassing one in the presence of others, was to ask for your opinion before giving his own, then, if he thought that you tended to politeness rather than truthfulness, he would give it you soundly when the others had gone. On one occasion, when some friends of the performers had brought a test record of one of his works for his approval, I gave a very non-committal answer in reply to his usual question. Afterwards, when we were alone, he said, 'Eric, you knew the playing was bad, didn't you ?' 'Of course,' I replied, 'but it was rather a delicate situation.'

'Nonsense,' said he, 'you knew it was bad; you should have said it was bad.'

What always amazed me was the way he coated his pills of truthfulness with the most disarming politeness, so that no one could really take offence. Would that I could convey some idea of the many difficult situations in which his wife and I were paralysed with the fear of what he was going to say next !

When strangers came, he would take no part in the first few minutes of conversation, unless he was addressed, but sit silent and aloof, sizing his visitors up in his mind chiefly by the sound of their voices. An unpleasant voice always had a disastrous effect on him, and he would long for the offender to go. It was usually the women who were at fault.

'Eric, will you please take that woman away,' he would whisper, when he judged she was out of ear-shot. 'I can't bear the sound of her voice any longer.'

His continual appearance of serenity – a serenity I always likened to the serenity of a lion as it sits gazing nonchalantly down at one at the Zoo – and his silence, ominous and full of awful possibilities, underlined his occasional remarks to a degree that had to be seen and heard to be believed.

There was no nonsense about him, nor would he tolerate it in others, and if he was bored he showed it pretty plainly. Even when dining with friends, if the conversation was not equal to the good food and the good wine, for which his table was renowned, I have heard him suddenly say to his man, with the un-mistakable accent of a Yorkshireman, 'Begin to read !' and his guests have had to sit in silence for the rest of the meal.

It is unlikely that I shall ever forget the visit of a certain violinist and his colleague, who came to Grez to treat the composer to their conception of his Sonata for Violin and Piano No. 1. Their stay was almost as brief as their rendering, for, in the silence of the turn of the page between the slow movement and the energetic last movement, a voice from the corner was heard to say, 'Good afternoon. Take me away, please, and, Jelka, make the lady and gentleman some tea !'

On another occasion, the visit of a famous string quartet who came to play Delius his own very un-satisfactory effort in that medium, and a very com-plicated quartet which Bernard van Dieren had just dedicated to him, the leader, embarrassed by Delius's aloofness and anxious to make a good impression, proposed that they should start off by playing one of the last quartets of Beethoven.

'Oh no, you won't,' came the response. 'Oh no, you won't !'

Woe betide anyone whom he found out to be a liar and a cheat. That person was never forgiven. I have seen Delius take an instant dislike to his man for no other reason than that he felt sure the fellow was not filling his glass to the brim. He knew the number of mouthfuls in a glass !

As I watched his servants feeding him, dressing him, and carrying him hither and thither, the thought struck me more than once how terrible it was that with his lively contempt for ordinary men Delius should be so pathetically dependent on ordinary men. Nor would he stop for a moment to chat with the kindly villagers whom we frequently met in the evenings on our way up the street, or returning from their work in the fields.

'If anybody comes up to us when we're out, take no notice, keep going,' were his orders when I first went to Grez. Never once did I see him unbend.

No workman was ever allowed to pass near him as he sat in the garden, and, if the electrician called unexpectedly to examine the wireless, he was not admitted until Delius had been carried away, or they had put a great screen round him. He remained an autocrat to the very end.

He set no store by the public taste. 'A few there

are who love and understand,' he would often say: 'they are the ones that count. The rest are not worth bothering about. To be a success in England you've got to be a second Mendelssohn. He gave the public what they wanted, "O Rest in the Lord." '

The sympathetic view to take is that he never understood the ordinary man because, so far as I can make out, he had never known the ordinary man. Once he had shaken the dust of Bradford from his feet, he seems to have associated with rather an odd sort of people, some of them very odd indeed, seeming to prefer that which was unusual in mankind to that which was normal. To hear him talk about the queer people with whom he had chiefly kept company during his formative years was always amusing, often fantastical. More than once he laughingly remarked that he wondered what some of the charming English friends his music had earned him would have thought about many of his former companions, most of whom appear to have been notable in various strange and unaccountable ways. In striking contrast to his turbulent youth, the Grez period in his life (1897–1934) was increasingly uneventful as the years went on save for the production of his works, until *le mauvais garçon de Montparnasse*, living more and more apart from his fellow men, gradually became the legendary recluse of Grez.

The root of the whole trouble was, I think, his horror of the mediocre.

I used to tell him that if he had ever talked to the ordinary man, as he pottered about in the little greenhouse of his allotment on his half-day holiday, he would have found him a delightful fellow. Shakespeare would have been in his element with the housepainter downstairs who, as I write, breaks out spasmodically into song: 'A hero I live . . . and a hero I shall die.'

Chesterton has put the matter in a nutshell: 'The first-rate great man is equal with other men, like Shakespeare. The second-rate great man is on his knees to other men, like Whitman. The third-rate great man is superior to other men, like Whistler.'

So we find that Delius's taste inclined to the particular in things, as in men, rather than to the general – to champagne rather than water, to the chromatic rather than the diatonic.

The fascinating northern dialect of a Grieg, the aristocratic and elegant utterance of a Chopin, he preferred to the common language of a Bach, a Beethoven, or a Sibelius. Being a man of excess, he exaggerated what in others was unessential. It had been so all his life. If he must smoke, then he must smoke all day long; if he was to have spinach, then spinach it had to be at almost every meal; if it was to be beautiful harmony, well, then, beautiful harmony it had to be all the time. There were no half-measures with Delius. In a man of less force and refinement such chromatic excess would have been positively harmful, as it was in Spohr, who lacked the strength and sweep of a Delius. Strength and refinement rarely go hand in hand; they are usually regarded as counter to one another; yet there are very few works in which these two seemingly opposite qualities are to be found in such measure as in the *Mass of Life*.

Refinement was a religion to Delius. I cannot recall a single instance of ever hearing him make a vulgar remark. He was as intolerant of bad manners as of ignorance.

'My boy,' he used to say, 'the greatest enemy you've got to fight in life is ignorance. You'll find it popping its ugly head up all over the place, and in places where you least expect to find it. I'm an old man now, and my whole life has been one long struggle against ignorance.'

That was the man as I knew him, hard, stern, proud, cynical, godless, completely self-absorbed – the man Frederick Delius.

Nothing could have so misrepresented the character of the man as the photographs which circulated through the Press during the latter years of his life, depicting him in the last and painful stages of a terrible affliction. It is a deplorable thing that these photographs were ever allowed to be published, for they have created in the public mind a legendary figure of the man which is as stupid as it is false. If, in this rough sketch of Delius, criticism be made by the few who knew him intimately that the drawing is a little hard, it must be conceded that the lines are true. If I have erred in this, I have erred in the right direction, for, though there was lovableness and a certain charm, the chief trait in my collected impression of the man is his severity. Such was the little I knew of Frederick Delius, a man of whom Nietzsche would have said, 'Here is one of the great despisers.'

What, then, of Delius the musician, and what of his attitude towards music ?

Strictly speaking, his attitude towards music is best defined by saying that he had no attitude. Music, for him, to use his own words, was simply and solely the means of expressing 'the imminent, unchanging realities of nature and humanity' as seen through the medium of his own individuality. The past, and the ideals and conventions of the past, whether they were of the classical order – the objective point of view – or the romantic order – the subjective point of view – occupied and interested him but little if at all. He was concerned in his own personal and particular way with the 'eternal present,' and that particular way he had not found by study, but by doing. No composer, with the possible exception of Verdi, was so unlearned.

From the very beginning Delius seems to have gone his own leisurely way, working through his influences, not avoiding them, firmly convinced that it was fatal to have more than a nodding acquaintanceship with the music of others. His development was unusually slow. It will always be a wonder to me how he had the courage to go on during his long apprenticeship, writing work after work in which there is scarcely a trace of the Delius we know, and not a hint of potential greatness.

At the same age at which Strauss had a *Don Juan* and Sibelius an *En Saga* to their respective credit, Delius was still plodding away at orchestral works which in their quiet moods plainly showed the influence of Grieg, and in their more vigorous moods the spell that the second manly theme in *Don Juan* had cast over him – the magnificent theme that is first given out by the horns. Forty years later he still revelled in that theme, and rarely missed an opportunity of hearing the work. I never hear *Don Juan* without thinking of Delius, and of the humorous way in which he used to tilt his head at the pedal G in the violins in preparation for the entrance of his favourite. Then, and at each appearance of the theme, he would all but wag his head off to its rhythm !

Delius was obviously one of those artists who only come to a full realisation of their powers after prolonged and unceasing application to their work, and that suddenly. It was not until he was thirty-seven that he produced a work that was greatly in advance of anything he had written hitherto, and which proved him a man to be reckoned with – his orchestral work *Paris, the Song of a Great City.* Yet, even so, *Paris* (1899) was not so completely advanced as to give the most discerning critic even the slightest suspicion of what was to follow in those six glorious years (1900–5) to which reference has already been made, to say nothing of his last period. How he found himself so suddenly is a mystery. That it was the effect of some strange inner happening or revelation seems the only reasonable explanation one can supply.

From now on he was sure of himself. He had never forced his work, but, guided first by his instinct and then by his intellect, had allowed his technique to grow unconsciously with his inspiration. He had laboured under one very severe handicap. Only twice during those difficult years of maturation had he heard the sound of his music on the orchestra, once at the age of twenty-six, and again when he was thirty-one. He had to wait until he was thirty-seven before he was able to profit to the utmost by such a necessary experience, and that on the occasion of the Delius concert at St. James's Hall, London, in 1899, which he gave at his own expense. He told me that after that concert he was so conscious of the faults of his music that he could not rest, but left London for Grez early the next morning, so eager was he to take up his sketches of *Paris* and apply the technical knowledge that he had just acquired.

Had there been the same opportunities in his day as there are in ours for the young composer of talent to get a hearing, I doubt whether he would have found himself any the sooner. No matter how technically proficient a man may be, his inner development can never be hurried. If a man has something worth saying, he will manage to say it somehow, no matter how clumsily. It is having that something worth saying that is the important thing. 'To be able to do something,' said Goethe, 'you must be something'; and, it seems to me, it was this suddenly 'being something' that accounted for the sudden and instant flowering of Delius's genius.

He was not one of those artists who are given to talking a great deal about their art, let alone solemnly, as so many of them do, and days would pass with not a mention of music. Certainly nobody would have guessed from his general conversation that he was a great composer. But I do remember his saying during a conversation about Walt Whitman: 'It was a long, long time before I understood exactly what I wanted to say, and then it came to me all at once.'

I have never heard of any artist who was so

completely and utterly himself, so detached and aloof from the world of his art and so little interested in the work of any other artist, past or present. It was not easy to gather very much about his views on the music of the past, for I soon discovered that the subject was unmentionable before him. Shortly after my first arrival in Grez, when there had been a relay of one of his works, I asked if we might keep the wireless on to hear a pianoforte concerto by Mozart. His reply was startling. 'You needn't ask me to listen to the music of the Immortals. I can't abide 'em. I finished with them long ago !' The only other remarks that I can remember are as follows: 'It takes a genius to write a movement like the slow movement in Schumann's Piano Quintet in E Flat, but the third movement is entirely without inspiration'; and, whilst listening to the Scotch Symphony, he commented, 'How much better Mendelssohn uses the orchestra than Beethoven.' He was indignant when he found that I was fond of Berlioz, whom he described as a vulgarian, and surprised that Debussy left me cold. *L'Après Midi* and *Pelléas* he loved, but detested the piano works. He had a glowing admiration for Bizet, whom he thought the greatest French composer, and he considered Verdi's *Falstaff* a masterpiece. Coming nearer our own time, he loathed Puccini, preferred the music of the Spaniards – Albeniz, Granados, and Da Falla – to that of the Russians – Borodin, Moussorgsky, and Rimsky-Korsakov – and enjoyed the records of Hebridean folk-songs from Mrs. Kennedy-Fraser's collection. What little interest he had ever had in the music of others a glance at his library will suffice to show. The only full scores he possessed were Beethoven's Symphonies (many of the pages are still uncut), the *Faust Symphonie* (Liszt), *Tristan und Isolde* (Wagner), *Don Juan, Til Eulenspiegel, Heldenleben, Zarathustra* (Strauss), *Rhapsodie Espagnole* (Chabrier), *La Mer* (Debussy), *Daphnis et Chloé* (Ravel); and Busoni's Pianoforte Concerto.

'It is a great mistake for young composers to study too much,' he used to say. 'People with a little talent nearly always kill it by too much learning. Learning kills instinct. It is just as dangerous as too much reflection.'

Despite his total indifference to the work and aims of others, he was ever ready to lend an ear to any young artist who was still struggling with himself. No young Treplev could complain of him, 'He has read his own story, but he has not even cut mine.' Often, when I was at Grez, he would receive music from quite unknown people, and when I had played it over to him, if it showed promise, he would return it with his dictated comments and kindly words of encouragement. If it showed no promise, it was ignored.

'You can't teach a young musician to compose,' I have heard him say, 'any more than you can teach a delicate plant how to grow, but you can guide him a little by putting a stick in here and a stick in there. Composition as taught in our academies is a farce. Where are the composers they produce ? Those who do manage to survive this systematic and idiotic teaching either write all alike, so that you can say that this lot belongs to this institution, this lot to that, or they give us the flat beer of their teachers, but watered down. In all probability those who are most aware of this depressing state of things are the teachers themselves. How can music ever be a mere intellectual speculation or a series of curious combinations of sound that can be classified like the articles in a grocer's shop ? Music is an outburst of the soul. It is addressed and should appeal instantly to the soul of the listener. It is not experimental analysis like chemistry. Never believe the saying that one must hear music many times to appreciate it. It is utter nonsense; the last resort of the incompetent. And another thing: the amateur musician is better without a knowledge of the science of music. When you see a lovely rose you treasure it as it is; you don't pull it to pieces to appreciate its beauty and find out where its delicious perfume comes from. So it should be with music.'

Here, waving aside the question of whether he was right or wrong, I will add, for what it is worth, that he always insisted that I should have been of no use whatever to him as an amanuensis had I not been practically self-taught.

Music, he thought, should be a simple and intimate thing, direct and immediate in its appeal from soul to soul, a thing of instinct rather than of learning, of the heart rather than of the head. It should never be complicated, or, in other words, the intellect should keep its proper place, for with complication music lost its power to move. One should never be conscious of its workings, or of how it was put together, otherwise how could it transport ? Some composers seemed to think that music was a means of displaying their ingenuity. Such an attitude was altogether unworthy of music. To be purely cerebral was easy. To be truly and genuinely emotional was hard. One should always feel rather than invent, and feel deeply, and never think out the detail of one's score. Much of the detail of modern music existed on paper alone, and could not be heard in performance. Even Strauss was not exempt from this failing.

The score of *A Village Romeo and Juliet* is a model of this effortless assembly of detail with the utmost economy of notes. The decorative detail, like the form, is not applied from the outside, but grows inevitably from the inside as the music proceeds.

Much as he resented adverse criticism of his work, Delius was entirely unmoved by it. It was his habit to have the various Press notices read aloud to him, and the unsympathetic criticism contained therein was almost always directed, not against the content of his music, as one might reasonably have expected from certain minds, but against what was called its 'lack of form.'

It has always been my opinion that Delius had a well-nigh perfect sense of form for what he had to say. In his mature works he said things as lucidly and expressively as he could. There is no 'passage-work,' no 'working-out,' no meaningless repetition, and in the sustained intensity of the rhapsodic flow of his music the decorative detail is caught up and transformed into the framework of his own particular sense of architectural design. I cannot see how he could have said what he had to say in any other way than the way he chose.

It is true that here and there he would have given more point to his charming discourse had he tightened up the form. The first instance that comes to mind is the slow movement of his Sonata for Violin and Piano No. 1, which actually ends several bars before the composer brings it to a close. Here, as in most instances, his sweet meandering is due not so much to his lack of proportion, but simply because he could not tear himself away from the loveliness that he had created.

Music has never been oppressed with loveliness, least of all in our time. It is ungrateful to complain of a surfeit of it in the work of one man.

Still, the fact remains that, although he sometimes nodded (he is in distinguished company here, for the very greatest have nodded at times), he had a much finer sense of form than his critics maintain. He is never formal, as even Mozart is sometimes formal, nor does he provoke one, as Elgar sometimes does, by his anxiety to keep the music going whilst he gets back somehow to that other theme that he has at the back of his mind. No matter what the method, a sustained intensity of thought is the aim of every composer. Delius's was that most dangerous and difficult method, the rhapsodic flight. The slightest failure of inspiration and down the machine came.

The remarks of his critics often gave him considerable amusement. 'Did you hear Beecham's magnificent performance of *Eventyr* ? ' he asked in a letter to me dictated to his wife. 'Jelka read a silly and superficial notice by one critic who said he was tired of counting the anti-climaxes in the work ! Fancy talking about climaxes and anti-climaxes in a work like *Eventyr*, a ballad based upon Norwegian peasants' fairy-tales ! The fellow still seems to have Beethoven's Symphonies as his *point de départ*, showing great lack of imagination.'

Once, after having read a particularly absurd criticism, he said, 'It is fatal with most of the critics if a composer has found it necessary to reject German forms and refuse to mould his thought into standardised patterns. One can't define form in so many words, but if I was asked I should say that it was nothing more than imparting spiritual unity to one's thought. It is contained in the thought itself, not applied as something that already exists. Look at Walt Whitman. Whitman spent his whole life writing *Leaves of Grass*. It is his individual contribution to art. Nobody else could have written it. So with my own work.'

Delius had no preliminaries in conversation, but always went straight to the heart of the matter. So it was with his music. Despite its 'wanderings as in dreams,' it is, at its best, and within the orbit of its own world, as direct and concentrated as is the music of Sibelius within the play of its own world. Reviewing his life's work, one can only wonder at the extraordinary richness of his imagination, and the astonishingly wide range of thought that world contained. It is a far cry from the romantic exuberances of *Paris* to the fantastic frolickings of *Eventyr*, from the song of a lover in the *Mass of Life* to the song of a lover in

Songs of Sunset, from the honeyed intimacies of the chorus in *Appalachia* to the sexless, impersonal voices in the wordless chorus in the *Song of the High Hills*, from the rich mellowness of *In a Summer Garden* to the comparative bareness and bleakness of the *North Country Sketches*, from the heartrending poignancies of *Sea-drift* to the exotic extravagancies of *Hassan*. How he managed to ring so many changes on the circumscribed musical stuff of his thought is evidence of the truth that it is only genius that matters.

It has always struck me as odd that with the innumerable evidences to be found in his music of a highly developed and extremely subtle feeling for sounds at work – the slow movement of the double concerto and several 'pictures' in the opera *Fennimore and Gerda* are miracles of loveliness when played with understanding, if we have ears to hear – Delius had no feeling whatever for the music of words. I stress the word feeling, for, as far as he was concerned, music was little more than the habit of feeling logically in sounds. It would hardly be an exaggeration to say that life for him was entirely a matter of feeling, for, as I have remarked, he was contemptuous of learning, and completely anti-metaphysical. Never once did I hear him say that this composer had an excellent melodic gift, or that composer a beautiful sense of design; it was always a reluctant admittance that 'Yes, that song shows fine feeling,' or, 'That passage is good. What beautiful feeling !'

Fine feeling had to mean precisely what he felt by fine feeling, and fine feeling meant vital harmony. He was entirely incapable of feeling a thing from anybody else's point of view, only from his own. The fine feeling exemplified in the tender delicacy of that gem of a slow movement of Mozart's Symphony No. 34 in C was abhorrent to him; the fine feeling such as we find in the strong, heavy brooding in the slow movement of Sibelius's String Quartet – the Beethovenish quality – he loathed. Nor was he moved by a fine melody that ran along easily and effortlessly, now quickening impulsively here, now relaxing in repose there, with but a bare understatement of its implied harmony in the basses and occasional interpolations from the middle voices. That sort of music-making he hated. For him, the power to stir, or be stirred, was always measured by the harmonic intensity of a work.

In setting words, however, it must not be imagined that he was careless. I have heard him declaim a phrase over and over again – but always, oh, so clumsily ! – before finding the music for it. It will, no doubt, astonish the many who, like myself, must often have flinched before his mutilations of English to hear that he used to say, 'I am always at my best when there are words.' That he probed to the heart of whatever poem he was setting is beyond the shadow of a doubt, but I am equally certain that he had no notion of how badly he declaimed English. Of his settings in German and Norwegian I am not competent to judge, but, with English, the words are almost like an unnecessary commentary on the mood which the composer has drawn up from the depths of their meaning. The melodic accent he imposes on them is wholly at variance with their verbal accent. One can more readily forgive this in a composer who is unwilling to sacrifice the shape and spacing of the beautiful melody that he has been at such pains to perfect to the shape and spacing of the words that he has been given to set.   In the case of Delius it was unforgivable, for it would have been just as easy for him to spread the words out comfortably and accurately over the rich texture of sound they had inspired in him as to perpetrate the verbal absurdities of an otherwise lovely work like *Songs of Sunset.*

I often gathered from his remarks, whilst listening to music with him, that he regarded voices in the nature of a necessary encumbrance.   There were certain works in which one could not very well do without them, yet they were a nuisance all the same. Often, during relays of his choral works in which one guessed that the microphone had been placed in such a position as to give undue prominence to the voices, he would say, 'Can't you get the *Orchester* any louder ?' (He always used the German form of the word.) 'It doesn't matter so much about my hearing the singers.   The *Orchester* – the *Orchester* is the chief thing I want to hear.' It was the same in listening to Wagner. 'Never mind so much about the singers, or even what they are singing about; the narrative is in the *Orchester.*'

What he did understand in writing for voices was the colour of choral sound, and the peculiar emphasis and choice of voice a particular line needed if it was to tell effectively in the harmonic texture.   He used to relate with great amusement how, at the early rehearsals for the first performance of *Sea-drift*, at the Tonkünstlerfest in Essen in 1906, they thought the chorus parts unnecessarily difficult, whereupon one bright fellow decided to rewrite several passages, distributing the parts in such a way as to facilitate their execution, yet preserving the actual harmony. After a great deal of manipulation he finished the job, convinced that he had done the composer a noble service. Copies were made of the new part-writing, and a few crack singers from the chorus chosen to sing the improved version, so that the indignant composer might be shown the error of his ways. 'When they had finished singing,' said Delius, 'I told my good friend that he could just alter it all back again; that I would have none of it! He had taken all the character out of my music. The outcome of it all was that he apologised, and said that it had been a shocking eye-opener to him. He would never have believed that such music could have sounded so different when the part-writing had been altered. When he heard the total effect of the chorus with the orchestra at the last rehearsals – and how thoroughly they used to rehearse in Germany in those days ! – he was more surprised than ever, and heard for himself that the chorus parts had to sound exactly as I had distributed them.'

The root of his insensibility to the music of words was, I think, a certain lack of literary taste. A man's library is usually a fair criterion of his mind, but, apart from the dozen or so books that had been given him at various times by Heseltine, whose taste was, of course, impeccable, there remained very few that one would have associated with a mind of Delius's quality and stature.

During the six years that I knew him I never remember his reading anything in English other than
autobiographies, both political and artistic, detective
stories, and any yarn, no matter what it was, that told
about the sea. So long as it was colourful, and the
action moved quickly, he was content. He had no
patience with a writer like Conrad, who took his time
in the telling of a story. Of English verse he knew
surprisingly little, and never once during my stay at
Grez did he ever ask us to read a line of it to him.
Several times I fancied that it would be an agreeable
change from our normal routine of book-reading, but
he always turned my suggestion down.

From 1895 onwards, with the exception of the text
of the *Mass of Life*, which was selected from *Thus
Spake Zarathustra* by Fritz Cassirer and the composer
during a holiday together in Brittany, the composer's
wife chose almost every word that he set. Whenever
she came upon a poem that matched the mood of that
sad longing which she had first sensed in his improvisation, she copied it out and left it on his desk.
Sometimes, she told me, the music he played was so
poignant that she thought her heart would break.
The granddaughter of Moscheles, she had been
brought up from her earliest years in an atmosphere
of music and culture. She had heard a great deal of
extemporisation in her youth, but none that bore the
slightest resemblance to that of Delius, either in
mood or manner. Whereas everyone else improvised
on easily recognisable themes, with Delius there were
no themes, just chords. When the mood to extem-
porise was on him, he always followed the same

procedure. He would start very quietly and dreamily, moving along slowly and, for the most part, chromatically in a rhapsodic procession of chords from one leisurely climax to another, until the music culminated in a tremendous outburst; then, with many tender dallyings by the way, it would end as peacefully as it had begun.

Delius, according to his wife, was a very bad pianist, playing his own music shockingly. His slender, tapering fingers were too long to play even the simplest runs cleanly. His limited technique had been a severe handicap to him all along, for he was never able to play his works from his scores when he showed them to various publishers. Yet, when he improvised, it was as if other hands were fingering the keys. Such improvisation, she said, was, in its way, quite as impressive as the more florid outpourings of the accomplished technician; to her ears it was certainly more musical.

It would have been interesting to have heard Delius improvise, for then it would have shown to what extent his improvisation had influenced his composition. He composed every note of his work at the piano (with the exception of the opening to the *Song of Summer*), and there is no doubt in my mind that his limited keyboard technique was largely responsible for the occasional mechanical chromatic slidings of his harmony, the oft-restricted movement of his part-writing, the frequent lack of fitness in his writing for strings, and the unrelieved, plodding crotchet movement of much of his music.

Although his music is instantly recognisable, it

has no style – style as it is generally understood in the sense of precision and ease of manner, trimness, aristocratic movement, and grace of gesture held to the point of perfect control. Such style is the pre-rogative of those artists who attempted none but the shorter and safer flights. It would be as absurd as it would be unreasonable to expect such a sense of style in the rhapsodic broodings of a Delius as in the rhapsodic violences of a Beethoven. Style rarely clothes the intelligence of a weighty mind.

No music is more difficult to interpret convincingly, or requires more rehearsal, than the music of Delius, and no music sounds duller when it is badly played. Consummate artistry and skill are needed to hold that simple texture together and give it life. Delius is like that delightful member of the team who goes in to bat fairly well down the list, and requires a great deal of fuss and attention. One must fasten his pads for him, help him into his batting-gloves, adjust his cap, and sometimes even run for him, but, somehow, it is worth it; he always manages to score. Some of his shots may be flukes, and, where a crack batsman would play a defensive stroke to a ball pitched well up on his middle stump, Delius, serene and unruffled, with a mixture of bat, pad, and glove will steer the same pitched ball dangerously through the slips for a boundary, then fall to a silly catch from a ball that he should have hit out of the field. And the amazing thing about it all is that it never once occurs to him that his escapades might give the others some anxiety, or that he takes more looking after than the rest of the team put together.

This music has a way with it all its own, and, unless that way is grasped instinctively and immediately, conductor, player, and singer alike might just as well shut up their Delius scores and give them away. The music of Delius is not an acquired taste. One either likes it the moment one first hears it, or the sound of it is once and for ever distasteful to one. It is an art which will never enjoy an appeal to the many, but one which will always be loved, and dearly loved, by the few.

I am at a peculiar disadvantage in being unable to say anything of consequence regarding the so-called English characteristics of the work of Delius. I can only speak of his music in relation to my own limited experience. A penetrating thinker like Cecil Gray has proved conclusively on paper that 'nothing could be more unmistakably English than such things as the Dance Rhapsody No. 1 or *In a Summer Garden*, or the two lovely pieces for small orchestra – in spite of the fact that the first of these two latter happens, quite irrelevantly, to be based on a Norwegian folk-song. How magically, too, do the first few pages of *Brigg Fair* evoke the atmosphere of an early summer morning in the English country, with its suggestion of a faint mist veiling the horizon, and the fragrant scent of the dawn in the air !'

Yet I cannot understand why it is that when I walk about the countryside of England I seldom, if ever, find myself humming anything of Delius, but always some exquisite passage from Elgar; either something from the 'Cello Concerto, the Introduction and Allegro for Strings, the String Quartet, the lovely interludes in *Falstaff*, the 'W. N.' variation, or the opening theme of the last movement of the Second Symphony.

When I am in France, and taking the same walks that Delius had taken for over thirty years, the walks on which he thought of nothing else but music, which, he told me, was ripening in his mind as the years went on, it is impossible for me to get that music of Delius out of my mind. I am singing it all the while. The gardens at Grez on a summer day, the river, the woods, that stretch of meadow opposite his house, that unforgettably beautiful walk on to Montigny, the mellow countryside round Villiers and Recloses, the rich brown soil, the indescribable feelings such as I have only felt at sunset up there on the road over to Marlotte – here, for me, was the source of his inspiration, not England. Even the wizardry of Sir Thomas Beecham cannot make me 'hear' England in this music, but transports me to the countryside round Grez. All the time I was at Grez I never thought of Elgar's music unless I was homesick.

I have not the learning to trace the artistic lineage of Delius, even if it were desirable in a book of this kind. It would require several years of profound study, an undertaking which very few young men can afford. It is all very well to point out that in such-and-such a work there is a suggestion of Grieg in the turn of a modulation, or Chopin in the shape of the melodic line, or Wagner in the sense of flow. These things are but the bait of the problem, ever ready to catch the unwary. Perhaps, in a more leisurely age, scholars will be able to show just how far an artist had been influenced by the work of others, and just how far similarities of expression are the workings of an unconscious affinity of mind. In all probability, in the case of Delius, such enlightened eyes may see no further than mine – that as Delius he began and as Delius he ended.

Whatever one's personal reaction to his music may be, no one can fail to admire his artistic integrity, which remained inviolate from first to last. In a short article written for a Polish paper some months before I first went to Grez, he had written, 'There is evidently something wrong with musicians who can suddenly change their entire outlook and experiment in atonal ugliness. Is the present tendency perhaps due to lack of imagination, a lack of emotion ? Is it perhaps the outcome of our hasty mode of life, or a striving after publicity, arrivism, sensationalism, or self-advertisement ? Is it an equivalent of cubism or futurism which seems to have already gone out of fashion ? It is difficult to tell. But I feel certain that no outward influences, no set principles or theories, can give birth to beautiful music.'

'No outward influences, no set principles or theories' – these words epitomise the man and the musician.

He would have agreed whole-heartedly with Verdi (that other born fighter, who, like himself, always went his own way) when he wrote, 'I believe in inspiration; you in workmanship. I admit your criterion as a basis for discussion, but I want art in all its manifestations – not amusement, artifice, system, which is what you prefer. Am I right ? Am

I wrong ? . . . My backbone is not supple enough for me to yield and deny convictions which are so deeply rooted. If artists could understand the meaning of truth, there would be no longer music of the past and music of the future, realistic and idealistic painters, classical and romantic poetry – but true poetry, true paintings, true music.'

To write true music a man must be that rare thing, a true artist. No artist of any age was more worthy of that epithet than Frederick Delius. Despite his negative and somewhat depressing outlook on life, the best of what he was still lives for our delight. So long as the noble art of music is held in reverence, so long will his music be played. His was true music, the glory of a great and imperishable name.

PART FOUR

THE SUNDOWN

IT may be remembered that I had left Grez in the summer of 1933 on the understanding that they were to send for me if need be, and I knew that, when that time came, it would be for no musical thing that I should be needed, but for something of greater moment, and the dread of that something – whatever it might be – was never far from me. I had often wondered how it would all end; whether Delius would outlive his wife, or whether she would suddenly break down under the strain of that constant watching and anxiety.

Delius had 'listened-in' to the first performance of the *Fantastic Dance* on January 12th (1934) under Dr. Adrian Boult. 'The weather conditions were not very favourable, but Fred was very pleased, and said that, as far as he could judge, it was a good perform-ance,' was the verdict.

Later that month there came a letter which read:

'23.1.34.

'Fred has been very unwell for nearly a week and has given me great anxiety. . . . I phoned at once to Dr. P—— in Paris and he said that if there was no fever or pain it was not immediately dangerous. But Fred's man was so anxious, and I as well, that we got the Nemours doctor to come. He put Fred on a very severe diet, and we had to keep him in his bed (oh !

the difficulty), cook all his food without salt, no exciting drinks, no fish or fowl, no milk, etc. You who know Fred will understand all that I was up against.'

Shortly afterwards I received another letter as follows:

'I have been so often to Fontainebleau for medicine, food, analysis at the hospital, that with all the reading I have to do now that Peggy has gone I really have not the time to write. But now Fred is much better, and I told the doctor I could not go on with that diet as Fred simply ate nothing, so we are normal again and he had cider for his lunch yesterday.

'Did you hear Beecham's concert? We heard it remarkably well. I had even called on the people who have motors that afternoon, and got them so interested and willing that the baker baked his whole bread without electricity, that the B——s and C——s pumped by hand to feed all their animals, and the butcher lady also turned off her motor. It showed plainly that most of these disturbances come from these wretched motors. *Eventyr*, Fred thought, was quite amazing; he had never heard it like that before. He was immensely pleased with *Songs of Sunset*, the suavity of the whole, Beecham's exquisite handling of the orchestra, and the fine singing of Olga Haley. He also thought *The Walk to the Paradise Garden* was glorious, stronger and more passionate than on our recording. I was happy to see Fred nodding so elatedly his head to the music.'

Another letter dated March 12th read:

'Fred is all right. We read more than ever. To-day we are to eat roast pork with the fat and crisp skin left on. I brought it from Fontainebleau and Fred is quite excited about it. There have been negotiations about it for three weeks. Fred takes great interest in his food now, and I think that is a good sign, although his forethought and imagination are always much bigger than his actual appetite.'

At the beginning of April I was alarmed to hear rumours that Delius was gravely ill. I wrote to Mrs. Delius at once. She answered immediately:

'8.4.34.

'MY DEAR ERIC, – No, Fred is not seriously ill, but we must be most careful. . . . The worst is that he is troubled with the most dreadful shooting-pains that return every day at the same hour (5 p.m.) and persist through the whole night if he does not take a calming medicine, which he generally does. But, of course, all that makes him feel weak and fatigued in the morning.

'We have had several visitors, and, as Fred has been unable to see them, you will understand how these rumours arose. There is no actual necessity for you to come, but it would be delightful and an unspeakable help to me. Why not come for a month? It would take Fred out of his groove, to talk music once more. I asked him, and he said spontaneously, "Oh, I always love having Eric here!" . . .'

It was not possible for me to leave there and then,

P

so I decided to pay them a visit in May. A week before the day on which I had arranged to leave there came a letter containing the usual list of things that Delius fancied. Two days later, on returning home from an evening walk, a telegram awaited me. Its contents staggered me: 'When are you coming? Am operated on to-morrow Clinique St. Joseph, Fontaine-bleau. Jelka. May 17th, 1934.'

I weighed the matter in my mind and saw that nothing would be gained if I set out that night. I would wait till morning, when possibly there would be a letter. It came:

'16.5.34.

'DEAREST ERIC, – I am afraid I am very ill; I have gone on till I could not any more. They are going to fetch me this evening and operate on me in a *clinique* in Fontainebleau. Please, Eric, be an angel and come here as quick as you can and stay with Fred and keep him company. I hope when they will allow it you will come to see me, but Fred is the principal thing. I cannot write any more, but please, dear, do not fail us.

'Yours affectionately,
'JELKA DELIUS.'

By the same post there came another letter from a neighbour urging me to come at once and take charge of the household, for the chances were that Mrs. Delius would never survive the operation, so critical was her condition, and that should she come out of the hospital alive, she would be an invalid for the rest of her days.

All the way on that hurried journey to Grez my mind was full of awful possibilities. Would I reach Fontainebleau before she died ? And, should she die, how should I manage with Delius alone ? Would it mean the complete sacrifice of all my youthful years ? I should have to stay with him to the end.

Little did I realise that I was being summoned to the death-bed of my friend, and that his wife was to outlive him by a year.

It seemed strange that of all my returns to Grez this day should be the most beautiful. Great white oxen tramped leisurely across the fields, dragging the enormous, top-heavy, two-wheeled carts that the French use, and here and there little groups of men, brown with the hot sun, rested under the fruit-trees, now in full blossom, eating their bread and cheese and drinking red wine from their bottles, whilst others in wide-brimmed straw hats bent their backs in the asparagus fields. My mind was not in tune with these good things of the earth, and I paid little heed to them.

I entered the house and went straightway to Delius's room. As he heard me mounting the staircase he called out, 'Eric, Eric, is that you ? Eric !'

'Here I am, Delius !' I shouted.

'Oh, lad, it's good to have you back; where are you ? Come here, come here !' he cried.

I went over to the bed and took the delicate hand he offered me and kissed his brow, for he was weeping like a child. As I stood there beside him I could scarcely believe my eyes. I had never seen him look like that before. He was much thinner, and but the shadow of that relic of a man I had known for these six years.

'What a catastrophe this is!' said he, 'Jelka so ill, and here am I left alone.'

He then went on to tell me how he had come to detest his male nurse because of his roughness and uncouthness; that he wanted me to share his room so that he could have me by him all the time. I muttered something about Yorkshiremen always pulling through, and that all would be well. Now that I was there, he seemed contented though weary, and was not disposed to talk even of his wife's illness. Would I read to him?

'Let's read *Huckleberry Finn* again!' said he. . . .

After about an hour of this the German nurse came in, bowed very gravely, as I continued to read, and, glancing at his watch and then at me, took up his German translation of an Edgar Wallace thriller, and began to read in a loud voice that startled the old man and drowned my efforts completely.

Realising that Mark Twain was no match for Edgar Wallace, I threw my book down, and, whispering to Delius that I would be back soon, rushed round by the church to see Mrs. Brooks, to find out exactly what had happened. The operation, she told me, had been successful. I might go and see Mrs. Delius in the morning. That was reassuring.

That night after supper I went up to Delius's room, determined to rouse him. 'Come, Delius,' said I, 'let's have some music on the gramophone.'

'Very well,' he replied, 'play me *In a Summer Garden*.'

I went downstairs and, turning the great horn of his E.M.G. gramophone towards the staircase, put on Geoffrey Toye's record.

That was the last music he heard.

He now seemed brighter, and we talked about music. Had I seen Beecham lately? I told him that I had, and about the magnificent performance of *Paris* that I had heard him give only a few weeks before at Queen's Hall. The old man was delighted, and said how he longed to hear the records of *Paris* and *Eventyr* that Sir Thomas was then making for the Delius Society.

'I have only one wish as far as my best music is concerned,' said he. 'I want Thomas to record it all.'

Delius, apparently, had no idea of the gravity of his wife's illness, and appeared to think that it was quite a minor operation, from which she would recover and be home again shortly to resume her normal duties. After every visit I made to Fontainebleau to see her it was always the same question he asked: 'Isn't she coming back to-morrow?'

With the days my difficulties increased. Backwards and forwards I went, keeping his condition from her, and hers from him, until at the end of a fortnight, the worry, suspense, and responsibility became more than flesh and blood could bear. The *pyréthane* which they gave Delius to ease the pain upset him so that he could not retain his food, and he was gradually growing weaker and weaker and could not sleep, even during the reading. I was now reading nine hours a day and the greater part of the night. Unless one read to occupy his mind he seemed to be in constant pain. Nor could he rest in any one position for long without my having to move him, or lift him up to take the folds out of his pyjama-jacket, which continually hurt his back. One could have done with an army of nurses, except that he would have dismissed the lot. He would now only tolerate his nurse at the most necessary times.

I begged Sir Thomas to send us the test records of *Paris*. Word came that they were already on the way, so we lived for the moment we should hear them. Sad to say, they were held up in the French Customs at Calais, and, though we wrote letters and sent telegrams explaining that they were not for sale, they were not released until after Delius's death.

After discussing the situation thoroughly with the Nemours doctor, and slightly with Mrs. Delius, who was now out of danger and making a splendid recovery, it was decided to invite the doctor's colleague, a very celebrated man who had lately come to Fontainebleau, to give his opinion on Delius. This, however, could not be done without a good deal of tact, for Delius would not have submitted to an examination without the approval of his wife, on whom he relied for most things to an amazing degree. Again, it was important not to alarm such a sensitive intelligence as his. To the credit of the two doctors and of Mrs. Delius, I am confident that he thought that this relapse was but of temporary duration. He would recover when she returned. Formerly I left the room on such occasions, but this time, when the doctors arrived, Delius said, 'Don't leave me, lad.' They stayed about ten minutes, and, as they glanced at one another, I read in their

looks that impersonal despair that doctors assume
when things look bad. Delius remained passive and
collected, answering their questions firmly, but when
they asked him about his sight he flared up in bitter
resentment. They then went downstairs, and remained in consultation for over half an hour, when
they returned and announced the course of treatment
they had prescribed. Taking me aside, the Fontainebleau doctor told me that at the very most Delius
could not possibly live for more than three months.
I lost no time, but immediately acquainted Sir
Thomas Beecham and Balfour Gardiner with what
had happened, and, as the latter was proposing to
visit Grez in July, I suggested that it would be a
tremendous help to me in this crisis if he could come
at once. This he most generously agreed to do, and,
waving everything aside, hurried to Grez.

Meanwhile Delius had rallied considerably under
the new treatment, and by the time his friend arrived
was greatly improved. Unfortunately, Balfour Gardiner could not stay for more than two days, but was
kind enough to promise that in the event of a further
relapse he would return. The companionship, understanding, and advice which he gave me during those
days made it possible for me to go on alone.

Shortly after Balfour Gardiner's departure Delius
became less well, but there was not the slightest
indication that death was imminent. We had come
to that part of Mark Twain's *Roughing It* which tells of
the adventures of the unmanageable Mexican horse,
and the old man had laughed and joked about it.
But I noticed that, as I continued, he became less and

less interested, and appeared to be sinking slowly into a coma. I summoned the doctor immediately. (One of the precautions that Delius had taken to preserve his privacy – his refusal to install a telephone – now became a serious handicap. The only means of communication in the night with the doctor in Nemours was the cook's husband, on his capricious motor-cycle. Having knocked this good fellow up – he was always willing to be of service – I would pace Delius's bedroom, waiting and listening anxiously, helpless to relieve him. Then, after an interminable time, there would come a roaring and sputtering noise up the street. It would grow louder and louder. 'Ah, they're here !' I would say to myself, and rush quietly downstairs to admit them. But the sounds would grow fainter and fainter. He was just starting off !)

The doctor came with his morphia syringe and soon there was calm, but when the effects of the drug had worn off, Delius became restless again and asked me to read. This I did until eight o'clock the following morning, when the doctor returned. There yet remained one chance of reviving him, said he. He would bring Mrs. Delius back from the hospital that morning. By mid-day she was sitting by him, in a wheeled chair, and I left them alone. It was obvious that Delius was sinking rapidly; that he had not the strength to talk. All he wanted was the soothing drone of a voice to which he need make no response. It must not stop; it must go on, and on, and on.

I wired to Sir Thomas Beecham, Balfour Gardiner, and Ernest Newman, informing them that Delius was gravely ill. Through the help of Alden Brooks and his • wife, whose kindness and thoughtfulness during this dreadful time were unlimited, an excellent nurse was quickly found in Nemours for Mrs. Delius. The house inside now resembled a miniature hospital. Each time he came to, Delius was in agony. The doctor was now coming every four hours. Towards evening on that day, Friday, June 8th, he was easier, and his wife was brought in to see him. 'Jelka, I'm glad !' he muttered when told that she was there, and smiled faintly. Later that day his suffering was so intense that his features became distorted, and it was as much as his nurse and I could do to prevent him from falling out of bed. Finally, after a night the unspeakable horror of which I shall never forget, the doctor paid his second visit in the early hours of the morning with his morphia syringe, and from six o'clock that Saturday morning Delius was as if in a sound and noisy sleep. All day long he lay there, his mouth wide open, and his stertorous breathing could be heard down below in the garden. The village clock struck twelve. It was midnight. Still there was no change. But for the heavy action of his breathing he had not moved for eighteen hours.

They had persuaded me to take some rest, and I had gone reluctantly and flung myself on a couch, telling them to wake me should he stir. At four o'clock that Sunday morning they roused me. 'Sir, he is moving again !' I rushed into his bedroom; the nurse said that it would soon be over. The others said, 'Speak to him.' I knew it was hopeless, but I bent over him and called, 'Delius, Delius, this is Eric !'

I had not seen Death before, and it had always been linked in my mind with doctor, priest, and tears, but when it came none of these attendants was present. Within five minutes he was as if dead, but when I undid his pyjama-jacket the heart was still flickering. I took his cold hand and felt it grow colder in mine. It was the end.

I went through into Mrs. Delius's room. The agonising gaze of that sick woman was unforgettable, as she gradually lifted herself up on her side to look at me. 'My dear,' I said, 'be brave. Delius is dead !'

She did not speak or cry, but sank back on her pillows momentarily dazed. By this time the doctor had arrived, and, after examining that human wreckage on the bed, he turned to me and said, 'Oui, Monsieur, il est mort !' He was to lie in the music-room. Mrs. Delius begged to be brought in to see him, so we carried her through in her little chair. She explained exactly how she wanted him to lie, and ordered Madame Grespier to go out into the garden and pluck roses. Soon she was back with a basketful, and we strewed them round him and left him there. It was now almost half past five and getting light, and, when I had thanked the doctor and seen him out, I went back to the ghostly silence of the music-room, and, kneeling beside the body of this strange and unusual man who had been almost a father to me since the day I had come as a raw youth to help him, I prayed that God would forgive us our sins and receive his soul.

After breakfast I sent telegrams to Sir Thomas

Beecham and Balfour Gardiner informing them of the composer's death, and Mrs. Delius, Brooks, and I then discussed the question of his burial.

It had long been Delius's wish to be buried in the garden of his house, but, as this was not possible, he had said that he would like to rest in a country churchyard somewhere in the South of England, for there the churchyards had always reminded him of those he had loved up in Norway. Yorkshire was too bleak and too far away from London, for there would be some who would wish to visit his grave and he would like them to place wild flowers on it. I remember how, having heard him say all this, I thought it so strange that this man who believed in the soul's extinction at death should have given so much thought – indeed, any thought at all – as to where they should bury his bones.

It was decided to make arrangements for a temporary burial in the graveyard at Grez until such time as Mrs. Delius was able to travel, and a suitable spot in England could be found.

That night we heard the B.B.C. announcement of his death, followed by that exquisite passage from the *Walk to the Paradise Garden* (page 228).

Looking out over the garden, as I listened to that music, I saw the world of music as he entered it, and the world of music, richer now by far through his legacy of loveliness, as he had left it. And I, being young and of that hard, cold, and materialistic post-war generation of those who know little or nothing of the world of which he had sung, but only of a world of shams and substitutes and devastations, felt a sense

of finality, distinct from personal loss, as if with this man the very Spirit of Romance had died.

The following day Mrs. Delius sent to Paris for a *mouleur* to come and make a death-mask, and take an impression of the composer's right hand. There being no one else to help, it fell to my lot to assist at these gruesome proceedings, and, when a photographer had been called in to take several photographs of the dead man, I was glad to see the last of these gentlemen. How horrible are the tawdry trappings of death!

The next afternoon, with the sun still high in the sky, we laid him to rest in the ugly churchyard which is reached after a few minutes' walk out of the village on that Marlotte road, the scene of so many of our evening walks.

It was the strangest ceremony I have ever seen, and never do I want to see another like it. Yet there was something about it – a something difficult to express in words – that was characteristic of the man Delius, who had always gone his own way, been true to himself, and steadfast in his particular attitude towards life and death.

There was to be no semblance of a funeral whatever, and, when I had seen the coffin safely into the garish horse-drawn hearse awaiting it at the door, I departed in the opposite direction to join Brooks at his house, leaving it to go its lonely way up the village street, unattended save for the bearers who slouched along beside it. Balfour Gardiner, Mrs. Brooks, and her sister had gone on ahead, and, skirting the village in Brooks's car, Brooks, Barjansky, Klemperer (an old friend from Paris), and I met them at the graveyard and waited there. When the hearse had passed through the gates, we instinctively assumed some sort of orderly procession behind it, and followed it round to where it now halted amid the rows of rusty iron crosses bedecked with artificial flowers and wreaths, all in the sickliest colours. The coffin was taken from the hearse and borne across the ground to the grave by the wall. We all stood back, not knowing quite what to do, and the bearers now put it down on to the planks beside the grave and, turning round, eyed us appealingly. Someone nudged my elbow, and I heard Balfour Gardiner whisper, 'You go, Fenby'; so I walked over to the graveside and gave them the sign to lower the coffin into the grave. This done, the bearers stood aside, and the rest, nervous and embarrassed, came over to where I was. We lingered there for several moments in silence, bare-headed, looking down into the grave, and I wondered what was going on in the minds of the others. Then we all walked slowly away, still silent, and the masons began their work before the filling in of the grave.

The villagers behaved admirably. There was no idle curiosity, no lining of the street. Not one of them came near the graveyard. They understood.

Several days later a heather wreath arrived from the Lord Mayor and citizens of Bradford. Delius's old gardener wheeled it up to the graveside on his barrow, and stood with his cap in his hand as I laid it on the grave in their name.

I remained in Grez for a few weeks longer, until Mrs. Delius's aged brother and sister-in-law were able to pay her a visit. I then returned to England, happy in the belief that she was making a complete recovery. Later that year she was well enough to come over to England, and, with the help of Miss Margaret Harrison, chose the spot at Limpsfield where Delius now lies. It was arranged provisionally that his body should be brought over and buried there in the May or June of the following year.

As the months of that year passed by, it was evident that Mrs. Delius was not maintaining her progress, and during the last weeks immediately preceding Delius's reinterment it seemed doubtful whether she would be fit to travel. So determined was she to attend her husband's funeral that nothing could dissuade her, even though it was necessary to take her by ambulance to Paris. That she was unable to do so after having already reached London was a tragic disappointment to her.

I had promised her that I would return to Grez, to witness the exhumation and accompany Delius on his last journey. The coffin was now housed in the mortuary in the graveyard, and, having seen Mrs. Delius off by train from Paris, I went back to Grez alone. Early the next morning, as I was standing beside the passenger motor-hearse bidding farewell to Brooks and his wife whilst the others loaded it with its heavy burden, I could not help remarking how wrong Delius had been when he had chosen to be buried in England. He belonged to Grez, and only to Grez.

My friends agreed with me.

And as I looked back and saw them standing in the middle of the road gazing after us as we drove up that Marlotte road o'erlooking Grez – his favourite walk for years in his active days, and the road on which he loved to be wheeled in his carriage at sunset in the evening of his days – I knew that I was right.

From now on a curious indifference possessed me.

It struck nine as we passed through Fontainebleau, and we judged that with luck we should reach Boulogne by six that night. Turning west just before entering Paris, we passed through Versailles and headed north for Beauvais. My two young companions sitting at the front of the coach – the chauffeur a fat, happy, red-faced little fellow dressed in green livery, and the undertaker, tall, effeminate, and painful in a tight-fitting black coat and enshrouded in an air of professional gloom – seemed highly solicitous for my comfort and entertainment as we rode along. Whenever we passed some object of interest, the

Qᴅ

latter turned round, and, pulling back the sliding glass door in the screen which separated us, called my attention to its peculiarities, and held forth about its history in a manner that suggested that he had once been a guide of some sort or another. When we reached Beauvais, he asked me if I wished to stop there for lunch, and, when I had assented, he showed me a great hotel to which, he said, English people usually went. I asked my friends if I might lunch with them instead, on condition that they came as my guests. They told me that they knew a little restaurant where we should get good food and good wine, and, having backed the hearse up a side-street and left it there, they showed me the way down some dirty alleys which led into a narrow street approaching the cathedral. Here we found our restaurant and entered. The meal was all they had promised it to be, and more! It is a rule never to be forgotten in France to eat where the French eat, not where the English and Americans eat. My companions were very talkative and interesting, and I learnt a great deal about their respective occupations. They were keenly interested in, and asked a great many questions about, the King's Jubilee, and about life for such as them in London. They said that people of their class had been greatly impressed by the loyalty and unity of the British Empire. Who was Monsieur Delius, and what did he do ? They had never heard of him. Several times during the meal I had shown signs of uneasiness about the hearse up that back street, and, when I suggested that I should like to slip out to see if it was still there, they roared with laughter. I told them sternly that it was no joking matter for me. My tall friend was bent on showing me round the cathedral. I might not pass by that way again. It was still very hot when we left the restaurant, and, leaving his mate to refuel the hearse, he conducted me along the narrow streets until, reaching an opening, we suddenly saw the façade towering up before us. My chief recollection is the delicious coolness that met us when we entered, and how I thought of the time when I had caught cold, or imagined I had caught cold, on coming from an icy little church, not far from Grez, into the great heat outside, and how Delius had said that it served me right. He hoped it would teach me a lesson never to enter a church again.

Passing through Abbeville, we reached Boulogne a little sooner than we had expected and made our way down to the docks. Here, after consulting some filthy ledgers, they examined my papers relating to the deceased, and with much ado finally stamped them. The coffin was now put into a packing-case by a Boulogne undertaker and his men and swung aboard the Channel boat. My companions of the day were now ravenously hungry, so we parted, they to a café near the docks and I on to the boat.

Shortly after nine o'clock, when the passengers had disembarked, the coffin was being lifted into the English hearse which awaited it alongside the boat at Folkestone, and soon we were on our way to Limpsfield. It was midnight by the time we got there, and pitch-dark. The vicar met us at the lychgate, the coffin was placed on a bier, and, with lanterns to guide us, we moved slowly to the graveside. The coffin was lowered into the grave, and the silence of the night broken by the vicar's prayer, 'Let light perpetual shine on them, O Lord, and may the souls of the departed through the mercy of God rest in peace.' The coffin was now covered up temporarily for the night with boards.

I will not write of the funeral service in the late afternoon of that day. Such people as may find this book of interest were, no doubt, all there, or will have read about it elsewhere.

For me, it was all wrong. If the shade of Delius looked down from the Elysian fields, he too must have seen that it was all wrong and that he had blundered. Better that he had been left in that cold graveyard at Grez, over there by the wall amongst the peasants whom he had known, than that he should rest with strangers in a strange place even in his native land.

They buried his bones at Limpsfield, but his spirit will ever remain at Grez, the home of his life's work and the country round which was his chief inspiration.

Whatever feeling he may have had for England, Florida, and Norway, Grez was his home, and Grez should have been his last resting-place.

The only thing that was right was that a few days later his wife should be buried with him. This had been his wish when the time came, and justly so, for her one aim in life had been the establishment of his genius.

And so our friendship came to an end, and with it the passing of a man the likes of whom I know I shall never meet again. Youth is a strange time, and the stuff of youth is stranger. How glad I am that I wrote that letter!

APPENDIX OF
SCORES

A Song of Summer

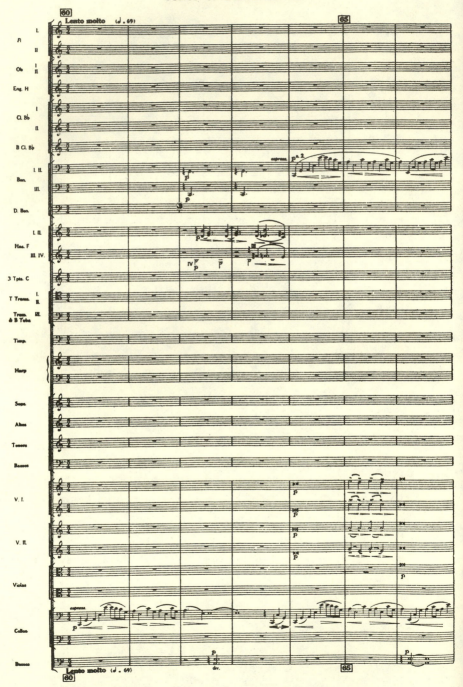

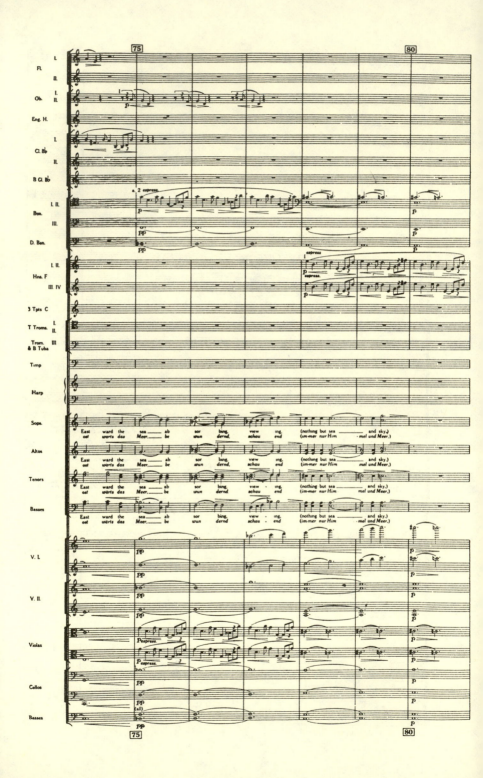

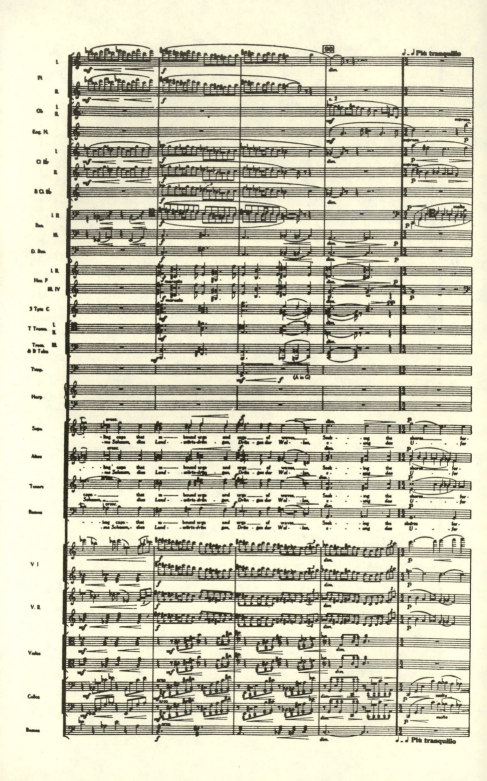

INDEX

INDEX

INDEX